LINCOLN CHRISTIAN UNIVERSITY

P9-CFY-956

CHRISTIAN WORSHIP IN THE PRIMITIVE CHURCH

121451

£6.95

62

CHRISTIAN WORSHIP
IN THE
PRIMITIVE CHURCH

BY

ALEXANDER B. MACDONALD

M.A., B.D., Ph.D.(Edin.)
Minister at Dron
Perthshire

Edinburgh : T. & T. CLARK, 38 George Street

1934

PRINTED IN GREAT BRITAIN BY
MORRISON AND GIBB LIMITED
FOR
T. & T. CLARK, EDINBURGH
LONDON: SIMPKIN MARSHALL, LIMITED
NEW YORK: CHARLES SCRIBNER'S SONS

FOREWORD

THE aim of this Foreword is simply to commend Dr. Macdonald's book both to thoughtful Christian people at large and to Christian ministers in particular, as deserving their special attention for more than one reason.

The place of Worship in the Christian life is now a very living, and for many even a pressing, question in the sphere of practice. This being so, a study of it in the setting of the Primitive Church, when Christian religion was most vital and least traditional in spirit, is highly relevant to the needs of to-day. It is just such a study that our author sets himself to furnish. But beyond this, his angle of approach and his method of treatment, as explained in the opening of his own Introduction, give his work a place apart from other books on Christian Worship, alike as an historical study and an interpretation from the inside. For there is, as he puts it, " a singular lack of books presenting a *unified* account of the Worship of the Primitive Church *as related to the spiritual experiences of the worshippers.*" The words I have put in italics contain the gist of his book's claim to special attention, as supplying what cannot really be found elsewhere.

In its execution, too, the present work is a fine example of " the historical spirit," which makes old things new by enabling men to-day to see them as through the eyes of those to whom they were living experiences, and so

v

objectively or as they really were. Moreover, it brings before the reader the results of the most recent research. But, above all, it adds to these merits a fresh touch of realism, by making all part of a unified, constructive exposition of Worship as organic to the spiritual life as a whole, when it pulsated with unique spontaneity in the Primitive Church. It thus recaptures the " vital " note characteristic of all New Testament facts.

It was for such reasons as these that I urged the writer, when his work came before me as an exercise for the Ph.D. degree in Edinburgh University, to prepare it for publication. And it is for the same reason that I now welcome this opportunity of giving it my testimony, alike as regards its timeliness and scholarly value.

J. VERNON BARTLET.

Oxford, 20th February 1934.

CONTENTS

PART I.

PRIMITIVE CHRISTIAN WORSHIP IN ITS GENERAL FEATURES

PART II.

THE WORSHIP IN DETAIL: WORD AND SACRAMENTS

vii

SUMMARY AND CONCLUSION

CHRISTIAN WORSHIP IN THE PRIMITIVE CHURCH

CHAPTER I

INTRODUCTION

THERE is a singular lack of books presenting a unified account of the Worship of the Primitive Church, as related to the spiritual experience of the worshippers. There is no lack of books which approach the subject from the liturgical standpoint, and make a careful study of the *forms* in which the Worship found its expression. But since the purpose of such studies is generally to trace the further history of these forms through succeeding centuries, and to find in the earlier practice an explanation and sanction of the later, the result is, that it is the forms of worship that command attention, while the worshipper himself remains in the background. The purpose of this present work is to place the worshipper in the centre of interest and attention ; and the main question asked about him will be : What was he thinking, and feeling, and experiencing, that he should have expressed himself during his worship in just these modes and forms ? The author has not come across any modern book, either in English or in German, which covers this ground ; and the present work is offered as a tentative effort to fill this notable gap. In essaying this task, a large debt has, of course, been incurred to many books, acknowledgment of which is made in the Bibliography. Of these some deal with the general history of the Church's life in its earliest period, others with individual features of the Worship.

I

Our main source of evidence for this study is the New Testament itself ; though the subsequent writings of the Sub-apostolic Age will often be appealed to as providing reliable clues where the New Testament itself has been silent, or as elucidating Scripture references which, by themselves, are indefinite and vague. At first, the New Testament books are apt to surprise and discourage us by their scantiness of reference to the worship-practices of their day, and to make us doubtful of the propriety of attempting any comprehensive account of these on a basis of evidence that is generally so slender. On the other hand, as we read the New Testament afresh with minds alert for traces of the Worship, we become increasingly aware that though it is not often mentioned, yet it is everywhere present behind the writers, giving form and colour and vitality to their modes of expression and thought ; and ere long we reach the conclusion that their frequent silence regarding their worship must be due in great measure to the largeness of the place it filled in their lives. They speak so little about it for just the same reason that we speak and think so little about the air we breathe. Their worship was a simple and natural function of their existence as Christian men ; and they saw no reason for pausing to describe a practice which to them and to their readers was familiar and matter of course, because so vitally a part of themselves. We shall have frequent occasion to verify this fact of the commanding influence which Worship exercised on the life and thought of the early Church.

The New Testament writings are marked by an unrivalled freshness, vigour, and power. Now, if their authors could write in this high strain, we may be certain that in this high strain they also worshipped. Within them dwelt a surging life of new thought and emotion ; the most astounding things had happened to them ; a deep thankfulness and an irrepressible joy possessed them ; and their worship came from them much as its full-throated song comes from the bird—as the simple, spontaneous, overflowing expression of an exuberant life that must of necessity have outlet. It may therefore be said, quite firmly, that we do not begin really to understand their worship until we approach it thus, from within. As the centuries advanced, its outward forms were to acquire an increasing importance ; for these came to possess a marked significance of their own, thanks to the larger store of thought, the finer artistry of word and phrase, and the accompaniments of movement and action, with which they were now enriched and adorned. But when we go back to the earliest period of all, with its surge of new-found life, the study of forms, though still important, is strictly secondary. When people are under the stress of deep and vivid emotions, they are not given to punctilious concern about the precise modes or forms in which to express themselves ; and there is no reason to think that the first Christians were exceptions to the rule. There is nothing to suggest that they had any liturgical theories to which they made their practice conform ; they certainly created no new worship-forms of their own ; all that they did was to take over, chiefly from the parent religion in Palestine, certain simple and familiar forms, or models, which they found to be adequate for their needs. In truth, their interest in such outward things as forms and ceremonies could only be secondary, in presence of the overwhelming inner experience that was flooding their lives from on high.

A prominent landmark in the history of Christian Worship is the Sunday's Service described by Justin the Martyr about the year A.D. 150. Justin was a very live Christian evangelist and thinker in Rome at the period when Antoninus Pius was Emperor ; and knowing the Emperor to be a man of broad and philosophic outlook, he addressed to him an *Apology*, or Defence of the Christians, in which he described their manner of thought and life, in the hope of disarming the slanderous reports that were circulating against them, and so of tempering the sternness of the Imperial attitude to their cause. Very fortunately, this *Apology* has been preserved to us. Among

other things, Justin gives the Emperor a brief description
of the Sunday-worship that was then current ; and his is
the first account that we possess of a complete Christian
Service. There are two striking features in this Service
of Justin's time. First of all, the framework of it is
identical with that of the Eucharistic Service common all
over Christendom to-day. The Service begins with the
familiar elements of the Reading of God's Word; an
Exhortation, or Homily ; Prayers ; and though Praise is
not mentioned, we know from other sources that by this
time Psalms and Hymns were features of the worship. This
part may conveniently be called the *Word-of-God Service* ;
and in substance it is the ordinary Sunday Service familiar
to many Protestant churches to-day. Then, without any
break or pause, there follows the celebration of the Lord's
Supper, or Eucharist. Here, then, is the first striking
fact. Already, by the middle of the second century,
Christianity had struck out its classic form of Sunday
Service and laid down the framework for the worship of
the future ; for though varied and even surprising developments were destined to appear in the course of the centuries,
these all took place *within* this simple framework, which
has never been superseded. The other striking fact is,
that this Sunday Service which our religion had thus early
established as her standard type is simply a juxtaposition
of the two Primitive elements of worship with which she
had started on her career. The Word-of-God Service had
been taken over as it stood from the Jewish synagogue ;
while the Lord's Supper also had its Jewish antecedents
and had been observed from the first. That is to say, in
the general forms of worship there was no marked change
during our period ; the advance—which was indeed great—
was in the *content* of thought and experience which were poured
into these old forms. This is not the place to embark on
the interesting but wide-reaching question of the uses of Art
for the expression and presentation of the Christian faith.
Enough to indicate as a historical fact the relative poverty
in artistic creation displayed by the earliest Church.

But while her creative impulses did not express themselves in the fashioning of new forms and ceremonies of
worship, they were directed, with a quite unique vigour,
upon the fresh spiritual content that was poured into the
old forms. Always it is the beginning of a religious movement that, as regards intrinsic vitality, marks its highest
achievement ; and it can scarcely be questioned that the
first generation of Christians evinced a higher creative
power than their successors in any age have done. In that
first period, extending roughly to about the year A.D. 70,
there emerged those classic products of Christian *literature*,
and Christian *thought*, and, above and behind these, of
Christian *experience*, which succeeding centuries were to
amplify and enrich and adorn, but which no succeeding
century was to transcend. In our present inquiry we shall
have frequent occasion to observe this remarkable creative
energy at its work. Perhaps nowhere is it more impressive than when we observe the young churches as they
yielded themselves up in their worship-assemblies to the
control of the Spirit of God, and, trusting to it wholly,
adventured out on uncharted seas of spiritual experience,
where they discover, once and for all, that in Christ they
have encountered the very power of God Himself, and in a
form adaptable to every sphere of their living. And right
at the centre of this vivid and fruitful activity, giving it
direction and inspiration, there stood the daily or weekly
Worship, conducted in its simple borrowed forms ; which
however became filled, at times almost to bursting-point,
with the surging tides of new thought, and emotion,
and experience. All this, and much more, can be seen in
our Primitive period. It will be upon this uniquely creative
period that our attention will be mainly focused ; yet care
will be taken to indicate, and to elucidate, the various lines
of development which ran out from it into the later New
Testament period, and on to the middle of the second
century.[1]

[1] This method will involve a less careful treatment of some
aspects of the *later* New Testament worship ; for instance, there will

It may be of service, at this point, to give a brief indication of the method and order of treatment adopted.

The two opening chapters carry us to the heart of the
subject. In the first of them an endeavour is made to
get inside a typical worship-gathering in one of the
Pauline churches, where we are at once arrested by the
pervading spirit of warm human *Fellowship*. When
we proceed, in the second, to survey this Fellowship in
its more distinctively religious aspects, we are introduced
to the two cardinal worship-phenomena of the *Spirit-
experiences* and the *Fellowship with Christ*. The fourth
chapter deals with a resultant of the social and religious
fellowship, namely, the note of *Joyous Confidence* which
rang through the worship. In the next chapter, a closer
estimate is given of the experiences and manifestations of
the Spirit, with their consequences of an inward *Enthusiasm*,
and an outward *Freedom* in the modes and forms of its
expression. It is claimed that we would be spared much
controversy about early Church Government and Orders,
if this dominating control by the Spirit were more justly
acknowledged. In Chapter Six, the survey of characteristic features is brought to a close in a *Historical Sketch* of
the Forms and Customs of Worship during the New Testament period. This sketch of outward development works
towards the *terminus ad quem* of the Sunday Service of
Justin's time, and is supplemented by a review of the
Waning of the Enthusiasm, with its far-reaching consequences in the systematising and standardising of worship-
practice.

be no serious attempt to estimate the penetration of worship-
thought by the mystical and immanental tendencies of the Hellenism
of the time. This whole question, along with the Johannine
worship-conceptions, is too large and delicate to be treated in
passing. It will be seen from frequent references that the author
regards the penetration by these extraneous influences as never
more than circumferential during the creative period of the Apostolic
Age, when the Jewish influence appears to have retained its control.
By the end of the century the penetration by Hellenism was becoming
more marked.

After these chapters, which survey the whole Worship in its general features and distinctive qualities, the next eight chapters deal, in detailed fashion, with its various elements. These are treated mainly in the order in which they appear in the classic form of Sunday Service. Baptism is reserved to the last, since that rite, being designed primarily for the individual, lay somewhat aside from the main current of the community's worship.

The closing chapter is a general but an important one. It summarises the conclusions reached as to the central place which the Worship held in the life and thought of early Christianity. Then follows an estimate of its influence on the growth of the Church's Thought, and of the method by which it was exercised. Lastly, and more particularly, its influence on the development of Christological thought is shown ; in which region the Lord's Supper would appear to have played a decisive rôle.

The only thing in this synopsis which calls for further notice is the treatment of the Lord's Supper.

Without serious question, the Lord's Supper was the culminating point of the whole worship ; and three chapters are devoted to it, with a supplementary chapter on the Eucharistic Prayer. Of late, there has been real progress in our understanding of the origin and early history of the Supper as a rite of the Church. In particular, Professor H. Lietzmann of Berlin, by his publication in 1926 of *Messe und Herrenmahl*, has appreciably advanced the front-line of inquiry. Bringing to his task an impressive equipment of historical and liturgical scholarship, Lietzmann adopts the method of working from the later Liturgies back to the original New Testament practices out of which, ultimately, these Liturgies have grown. He discovers, in these later Liturgies,[1] clear surviving traces of *two* distinct forms of celebration of the Lord's Supper in the early Church ; the earlier of these being

[1] Particularly the Liturgies of *Hippolytus* (c. A.D. 200) and of *Serapion* (c. A.D. 350).

what he calls " the Jerusalem type of Supper," referred to
in the New Testament as " the Breaking of bread " ;
while the later form is " the Pauline Supper," as described
in the eleventh chapter of *1 Corinthians*.   In this present
study of the question, Lietzmann's main conclusions are
adopted, though the line of approach to them differs from
his, in so far as it is based primarily on the New Testament.
At first sight, some may regard these conclusions as sub-
versive of much that has been peculiarly sacred ; but the
reader is begged to suspend judgment until the whole
position has been unfolded.   This new hypothesis certainly
entails a readjustment of historical perspective ; but, in
the author's own experience, it entails no spiritual readjustment, nor does it seem to him to impair, in any
degree whatever, the validity or the sacredness of the
celebration.   Those whose leanings are towards emphasis
upon ritual may not agree with this estimate of the character of these conclusions ; but the author can only say
that, for himself, as one whose duty and privilege it is to
preside at the celebration of the Lord's Supper, the new
historical perspective has invested the rite with a reality,
and the act of its administration with a feeling of confidence, which were sometimes found to be lacking amid the
historical haze which the old and familiar hypothesis
seemed unable to dispel.   No claim is made for these new
conclusions that they are final.   What is claimed for
them is that they appear to fit more of the facts than does
any other hypothesis, and that they offer a promising
starting-point for further inquiry.   In any case, Lietzmann's researches have already been widely recognised to
be a notable and reverent contribution to a difficult and
vital question.

No endeavour will be made, throughout this work, to
draw morals for our conduct of worship to-day.   Into
this modern problem other elements enter besides the
historical factors which are mainly to engage us now.
But there are two considerations of a more general kind

which, as a result of our inquiry, seem to thrust themselves
on our attention.

In the first place, one feels constrained to deprecate all
facile suggestions for a simple return to-day to the spirit
and methods of the Worship of the Primitive Church.
Even if our knowledge of that great Worship were more
sure and more detailed than it is, it would still be highly
doubtful if a return to it could ever be possible. We
might hope for a recovery of the early worshippers' sense
of the immediacy of the Spirit's action, but hardly for the
recapture of that exhilarating sense of *newness*, which
must have been a vital element of their vivid experience.
It should never be forgotten that even this great Apostolic
Church was unable to maintain itself, for much longer
than a single generation, upon the high levels of a free,
spontaneous, Spirit-controlled worship, and by the end
of the century was quite definitely moving down towards
those less exalted levels on which the Church has lived
and moved ever since.

The other, and more positive, consideration is thrust on
us by the feature of objectivity which we shall find to be
so marked in the early Worship. It was *objective* worship,
in the sense that the worshipper's mind became habituated
to an objective poise—to an adoring, contemplative gaze,
directed, not inwards, but outwards ; and it was objective
worship also in the deeper sense that it was believed to
accomplish something actual, something objective, as
between man and God. The Roman Catholic Church has
retained a strong hold upon her worshippers by reason
of the objectivity which pervades her celebration of the
Mass. For those who can accept its presuppositions, that
solemn act of worship draws much of its impressive power
from the conviction that, when the Mass is celebrated,
something *happens*, something is actually done, a real
transaction is completed between earth and heaven—
between God and man, between man and God. There will
not be found in this present work any plea on behalf of
the distinctive system of thought which lies behind the

Roman Mass. But there will be found much to suggest that we who are Protestants might with advantage import into our own worship more of this element of objectivity, and so recover a note which rings out very clear in that greatest of all earthly Worships, the Worship of the Primitive Church. With advantage, we might foster more carefully the spirit and mental attitude of adoring contemplation, and of adoring thankfulness and praise; and we might further consider how better to throw emphasis on the fact that, in our worship also, something happens, something is actually done, *an offering is made to God.*

PART I

PRIMITIVE CHRISTIAN WORSHIP IN ITS GENERAL FEATURES

CHAPTER II

THE WORSHIP AS FELLOWSHIP: ITS SOCIAL ASPECT

LET us picture the Christians of some Pauline church in a Gentile city as they gather for their worship. A few are people in good circumstances, but for the most part, if Corinth may be accepted as typical,[1] they are humble men and women—housewives, artisans, merchants in a small way, labourers, and even a few slaves. All day long they have been tied to their tasks, isolated in a world which cares nothing about the new interest that has transformed life for them, making all things new. But now that it is evening, they are free to follow the bent of their desires, and they make their way to where they know they will find brothers of the faith. Nor do they come with empty hands, except in the case of a few, and these the very poorest; for each carries a parcel of food, selected no doubt with careful thought, and purchased, it may be, with the coin of sacrifice. It is their contribution to the evening meal which all will share together; the richer brother the happier in that he is able to make up for what the poorer brother could not bring, and the poor brother glad to share from his neighbour's store, seeing it is offered in the love of Christ. *Agapê*, " Love-feast," they learned to call this meal; and if Tertullian [2] is right, they called it so because it displayed their Christian love in action.

Arrived at their place of meeting—some lecture-hall in

---

[1] I Cor. i. 26.   [2] *Apology*, 39.

a quiet street, or more likely some private house where a better-circumstanced brother lives, they greet each other with a kiss. Paul speaks of it as a " holy kiss " ; [1] Peter as the " kiss of love." [2] How far it was differentiated from the ordinary kiss of greeting, we do not know. [3] We may assume that it gave expression to the feeling that the brothers were members of one family, and that all un-brotherly impulses were left behind. Anyhow, we can scarcely exaggerate the warmth of this fellowship that was initiated with a kiss ; nor can we hope to emulate it— we with our colder northern blood and our cooler modern faith.

It is illuminating to learn that social fellowships, such as the Christian churches offered, were things that made instant appeal to the mind of the age.

" The organisations of the earliest churches were visible embodiments of such social ethics as fairly filled the soul of ancient man with enthusiasm."

In these words Deissmann [4] refers to a remarkable phen-omenon that was widespread in the Græco-Roman world, an illuminative account of which may be found in Dill's *Roman Society from Nero to Marcus Aurelius*, in the chapter on the " Colleges and Plebeian Life." These *colleges*, or guilds, sprang up in the first instance in the sea-ports and trading centres, where foreigners drew together in order to render mutual assistance, and to maintain the religious traditions of their homelands. But the move-ment had spread irresistibly into every craft and every town ; sometimes several guilds were to be found in a single street, so powerful was their attraction for the masses of artisans, labourers, merchants, and slaves who at that

[1] 1 Thess. v. 26.

[2] 1 Pet. v. 14.

[3] It is probable that at first the kiss was a kiss of greeting on arrival at the place of worship. Later, it was incorporated into the worship. Cf. *infra*, p. 34.

[4] *Light from the Ancient East*, p. 390.

time were experiencing an imperious need for human fellowship. The Roman Empire, in destroying the national and civic institutions, had broken up the old loyalties and left the individual in isolation, with a vacuum at his heart which he naturally sought to fill through voluntarily formed associations with his kind.

" In the face of the world-wide and all-powerful system of the Empire the individual subject felt ever more and more his helplessness and loneliness. The imperial power might be well-meaning and beneficent, but it was so terrible and levelling in the immense sweep of its forces that the isolated man seemed in its presence reduced to the insignificance of an insect or a grain of sand." [1]

In the guilds the individual regained his self-respect and found a satisfaction for his craving for sympathy and mutual succour.

" When the brotherhood, many of them of servile grade, met in full conclave to transact guild business or to regale themselves with a modest repast, or when they passed through the streets with banners flying, and all the emblems of their guild, the meanest member felt himself lifted for the moment above the dim hopeless obscurity of plebeian life." [2]

These guilds became homes for the homeless, a little fatherland for those without a country. They were all more or less religious, many of them being associated with one or other of the Mystery-deities that were flooding in from the East. The members hailed each other as *brothers*, a term which had thus acquired a religious sense before it appeared in the New Testament. It has been suggested that we might usefully think of these guilds as occupying in men's lives the place that would be taken, for a working man of to-day, by his Trade Union, his Masonic Lodge, his Friendly Society, and his Free Church—all rolled into one.

[1] P. 256. [2] P. 256.

This survey of the Guild-movement is relevant as helping to explain the ready sympathy which the common people seem from the first to have extended to the appeals of the Christian fellowships. Outwardly viewed, it was no violent transition to pass from a Roman *collegium* or a Greek *thiasos* to one of the *ecclesias* of Christianity. Socially, the aims of the guilds and the churches were largely parallel, and when the Church's expanding work called for machinery and organisation, it is possible that she borrowed suggestions from the riper experience of the guilds. One service the guilds did certainly render to the Church. By meeting the craving for fellowship they nurtured and developed it, and so prepared the way for that intenser warmth of fellowship which the Christian churches evoked.[1]

The New Testament is astonishingly rich in material which demonstrates the warmth and inward depth of the fellowship among the Christian brothers ; so much so that many moderns have singled out the *enthusiasm of humanity* as being the most distinctive quality of the new movement. Love is set forth in the New Testament as the chief of the Christian graces, and the bond that makes all cohere ; and when Paul writes to the Thessalonians that there is no need for him to give them injunctions about brotherly love, because " you are yourselves taught by God to love one another," [2] we infer that love was the quality, above all others, that was seen to spring up spontaneously and inevitably when a man became a Christian.

We confine our attention to a few of the more tangible manifestations of this love. From the earliest Jerusalem days a common fund was in existence for ministering to the needs of the distressed. Some, like Barnabas, threw all their possessions into this fund, laying them at the feet of the Apostles to be administered for the common good. The first officials that the Church elected were

[1] See J. Weiss, *Commentary on 1 Corinthians*, Introduction.
[2] 1 Thess. iv. 9.

chosen expressly to administer its charities, lest any be
overlooked.[1] Widows and orphans were a standing care ;
the sick, the distressed, the prisoner, the stranger, were
sought out and drawn within the circle of the Church's
beneficence. With increasing regularity and system,
local churches contributed not only for their own poor
but also for their Apostles and for the mother-church in
Jerusalem.[2] Ignatius may be cited as a witness for the
later New Testament period.[3] Though he was a man
much preoccupied with questions of episcopal order and
authority and deeply distressed at any breach in the Body
of Christ, yet even he makes it his final count against the
schismatic heretics that

> " they have no care for the poor, none for the widow,
> none for the orphan, none for the afflicted, none for
> the prisoner, none for the hungry and thirsty."

And all this warm philanthropy was most closely associated
with the worship. To the assemblies of the brothers it
owed not only its inspiration, but to a large extent also its
execution. We have an evidence of this in the worship-
practice of the second century, when the common meal
had been relegated to a subordinate place, and the worship
had shifted its centre to the Sunday Service as described
by Justin. Into this new and definitely ritual framework
the ministration to the needs of the poor was carried over
as an integral part of the Service. It came immediately
after the celebration of the Eucharist. Harnack [4] has re-
constructed the procedure : what follows is a summary of
his reconstruction.

Each Lord's day,[5] or once a month,[6] or when one
felt moved, gifts in money or in kind [7] were brought

---

[1] Acts vi. 1–6.   [2] Especially 2 Cor. viii., ix.   [3] *Smy.* vi. 2.
[4] *Mission und Ausbreitung des Christentums* (1902), p. 113.
[5] 1 Cor. xvi. 2.   [6] Tertullian, *Apology*, 39.
[7] " Early canons suggest that a Christian Eucharist in the first age
must have frequently resembled a modern harvest thanksgiving "
(Gore, *The Body of Christ*, p. 172).

to the worship and handed over to the President.
He laid them on the Lord's table, thereby consecrat-
ing them to God. The President decided who was
to receive, and how much; though he might be advised
by the deacons, who would be more familiar with the
needs of each case. Then the deacons distributed
the gifts to such recipients as were present, and, after
the worship was finished, conveyed the remainder
to the absent at their homes. From the first the
President appears to have had the supreme disposal
of the gifts, the deacons acting as his executives. The
powers and responsibilities involved were great;
hence the need that such men should be no lovers of
money.

These warm social contacts and philanthropies of the
early Church were a consequence of its fellowship being
fundamentally a religious one, and, strictly speaking, we
should have studied the cause before considering its
effects. But the reverse method, which we have adopted,
has two advantages. First, it enables us to observe the
worship from the same line of approach as it was observed
by many of those who came to it for the first time. Among
the strongest appeals which early Christianity made to
the outsider was its human warmth and the solidarity of
its fellowship; and it is probable that some of the new
converts were held loyal, during the early stages of their
adhesion, as much by the ties of brotherhood as by the tie
of devotion to the unseen Lord. Secondly, our method
throws emphasis from the start upon the unique way in
which the Worship was interpenetrated by social and
philanthropic interests. And this needs emphasis because,
not being familiar with anything quite like it in our modern
life, we find it somewhat elusive and difficult to grasp.
To-day, the social and philanthropic activities of the Church
are not initiated, and planned, and carried towards execution within the actual place of worship and in presence of
the worshipping people, but elsewhere, in church com-

mittee-rooms and halls ; and a very large part of our
Christian philanthropy is done through societies and
organisations which have ceased to have any official connection with the Church at all. But in the first Christian
churches it was quite otherwise. These small and compact
worship-assemblies which met, it appears, chiefly in private
houses, were the sole centres of early Christian life, and
were the reservoirs into which gravitated everything that
concerned the fellowship and the cause, and out of which
issued the streams of Christian effort and service. The
believers, we must remember, possessed nothing tangible
beyond their worship-assemblies. They possessed no
buildings : no sacred book that was distinctively their
own : no defined creed, nor any *rule*, such as Benedict or
Bernard left—nothing, except their worship-assemblies,
that could serve as a rallying-point for their loyalties.
The worship-assemblies were, in fact, the centre of everything.[1] It seems therefore that we must think of their
benevolent activities, whether directed to those within
the Christian circle or to those without, as being not only
inspired by the worship, but as being to a large degree
initiated, and planned, and in some cases carried into
execution, during its course. It may seem natural to us
to draw a distinction between the *agenda* in these assemblies
that were occupied with the more human and secular side
of affairs and those devoted to what we would describe as
the exercises of worship proper ; but it is doubtful if our
distinction would have commended itself to the worshippers
themselves. For there can be little question that they
thought of their meeting, with all its varied procedure,
as a compact unity, because controlled from beginning
to end by the Spirit of God.[2]

The above impressions are to be clearly gathered from

[1] See *infra*, p. 49. There will be found occasional statements,
especially in this chapter, which cannot be conveniently authenti-
cated till later, when we deal more with detail. Only the more
important of these will be noted.

[2] See *infra*, Chapter V.

2

those chapters [1] which Paul devotes to questions which arose in the worship at Corinth, and where every aptitude alike—be it an aptitude for engaging in prayer or one for ministering to the needy—is attributed to the self-same Source, namely, the Spirit of God. We get the same impression, though in a different way, from the twelfth chapter of *Romans*, where, from the third to the eighth verses, Paul definitely visualises the Romans as gathered together for worship, and then, at the ninth verse, his thought glides imperceptibly into the wider sphere of their everyday life, only to return, as at verse thirteen, to the worship-gathering. In other words, Paul does not seem to be aware of any clear boundary-line separating the two spheres between which his thought oscillates. Again, in writing to the Colossians, he is quite clearly envisaging them as gathered for worship when he says :

> " Let the inspiration of Christ dwell in your midst with all its wealth of wisdom ; teach and train one another with the music of psalms, with hymns, and songs of the spiritual life ; praise God with thankful hearts. Indeed, whatever you say or do, let everything be done calling upon the name of the Lord Jesus, giving thanks in his name to God the Father." [2]

In the last sentence, the thought very probably passes from the worship-gathering to the wider sphere of everyday life ; and again we are sensible of the absence of any clear line of demarcation between ritual worship proper and the service of God in practical things.

The truth seems to be that the New Testament conception of Worship was at once wider and more inward than ours. Moffatt remarks that " the three great definitions of Worship or religious service in the New Testament are

---

[1] 1 Cor. xi.–xiv.

[2] Col. iii. 16 f. Quotations from the N.T. will as a rule be given in Moffatt's *Translation*. Our minds are apt to glide too easily over the familiar phrases of the Authorised Version.

all inward and ethical." [1] The definitions referred to are
these :

> " I appeal to you by all the mercy of God to dedicate
> your bodies as a living sacrifice, consecrated and
> acceptable to God ; that is your cult, a spiritual
> rite." [2]
>
> " And by him let us constantly offer praise to God
> as our sacrifice, that is, the fruit of lips that celebrate
> his Name. Do not forget beneficence and charity
> either ; these are the kind of sacrifices that are
> acceptable to God." [3]
>
> " Pure, unsoiled religion in the judgment of God
> the Father means this : to care for orphans and widows
> in their trouble, and to keep oneself from the stain of
> the world." [4]

It is to be noted that, in each case, the significant Greek
word—*cult, rite, sacrifice, religion*—is a word that comes
from the old ritual worship. Perhaps we have a clue to
this mode of thought in the fact that Christianity stood
very near to the old sacrificial system, which, though
discredited in practice, had bequeathed the wholesome
idea that sacrifice was an essential element in true worship.
So it is probable that a cup of cold water given in the name
of Christ was looked upon, not merely as a thing well-
pleasing to God, but as evidencing a real approach of the
soul to God, as real as its approach to Him in prayer. Of
course, such a conception is not far removed from the
thought of good works as possessing in themselves merit
with God ; and it may have been a sense of this danger
that withheld Paul and others from saying anything quite
so definite as our Ancient Mariner's " he prayeth best who
loveth best." In any case, we seem entitled to conclude
that, neither in their thinking nor in the practice of their
worship-assemblies, did the early Christians draw as clear

[1] *I.C.C.* on Heb. xiii. 15 f. [2] Rom. xii. 1.
[3] Heb. xiii. 15 f. [4] James i. 27.

a line as we are disposed to draw between the Worship
of God and the service of man in the name of Christ.[1]

[1] Roughly speaking, it may be said that the high-churchman tends
to exalt the Church as being essentially *more than human*, while the
low-churchman tends to regard it as a means to an end, an instrument, a religious and social mechanism—and a mechanism, no
matter how fine it be nor how high its ends, remains, in itself, something *less than human*.   Over against these, the N.T., while doing
justice to both aspects, emphasises the intrinsic humanity of the
Church.   Alike in its triumphant joy in the Communion of Saints
and in the warm human fellowship of its worship, the N.T. Church
stands out as a profoundly *human* institution.   Cf. Sperry, *Reality in
Worship*, p. 28.

CHAPTER III

THE WORSHIP AS RELIGIOUS FELLOWSHIP

WE will assume that the Worship-assembly we are seeking to describe was of the type we shall find at Troas,[1] where the Supper-celebration was apparently preceded by a Word-of-God Service.[2] After the brothers had gathered, and had, probably at this point, greeted each other with a kiss, the President would begin the worship in time-honoured fashion by reading a portion of God's Word from the Old Testament, thereafter expounding its deeper meaning, or delivering an exhortation based on it. The President might be an Apostle, if such were present, or a Prophet, or a Teacher, or perhaps any member who had proved to be specially dowered by the Spirit. This, we may take it, was the essential qualification.[3] When the Reading and Homily were finished, the President would engage in Prayer, or, possibly, might invite some member to do so. After that, members generally would be invited to take part.

> " When you meet together each contributes something—a song of praise, a lesson, a revelation, a ' tongue,' an interpretation." [4]

Some one contributes a *song of praise* : by which is probably meant a hymn in praise of Christ, or of God and the Lamb, such as are preserved in the Book of *Revelation*. Another gives *a teaching*, an exposition of some definite theme— let us say, a Spirit-inspired interpretation of Scripture. Perhaps a Prophet rises, and with ecstatic fervour delivers *a revelation*—it may be of the future, such as Paul himself

---

[1] Questions of the order of worship are dealt with in Chapter VI.
[2] See p. 62 f.   [3] See Chapter V.   [4] 1 Cor. xiv. 26.

could give ; [1] or it may be a disclosure of the Divine Will
on some present issue, such as the choice of missionaries.[2]
Or perhaps the Prophet's aim is moral, as he seeks to
reach the consciences of his hearers.[3]   At Corinth we find
both the " private Christian " and the unbeliever present
at the worship, the former probably an adherent, though
not yet a baptized member of the Church.[4]   Paul gives a
vivid sketch of one or other of these coming into the
worship-gathering when a prophet is speaking ; and as he
listens, suddenly the Spirit-filled words take hold of him ;
they search his soul, and seem to be dragging out its
secrets and exposing them in the sight of all ; till at last
he falls on his face and worships God, exclaiming, " Surely
God is among you " [5]—an impressive index of the tensity
of atmosphere that must have been frequent.   Then some
other makes his contribution in prayer, Spirit-quickened
as all true prayer must be, and the whole assembly say
the *Amen*.[6]   It may be that the prayer is one uttered
under great stress of feeling in the form of a *tongue*,[7] in
which case it will be intelligible only to some gifted inter-
preter whose office it will be to give the *interpretation*.[8]
Perhaps the practice is already coming into vogue for the
whole assembly to pray together in unison,[9] though this is
highly doubtful as postulating some settled form of ritual.
Less improbable would be the antiphonal singing of praise
of which Pliny writes, and an example of which we find in
the heavenly worship of the *Apocalypse*.[10]   As to the manner
in which such praises were " sung " we know nothing.

Our materials for this picture of the worship are drawn
mainly from Paul's first letter to the Corinthians, which
may throw greater emphasis on the ecstatic elements than
was typical of worship throughout the Church.   At
Thessalonica the temperature was lower ; yet that coolness
did not find favour with Paul any more than did the

---

[1] *E.g.* 1 Cor. xv. 51 f.   [2] Acts xiii. 2.   [3] Cf. Ignatius, *Phil.* vii.
[4] 1 Cor. xiv. 23.   See *infra*, p. 182 f.   [5] v. 25.
[6] 1 Cor. xiv. 16.   [7] 1 Cor. xiv. 14.   [8] 1 Cor. xiv. 28.
[9] Justin, *Apology* i. 65, 67.   [10] v. 9–14.

excessive ardours at Corinth, for he counsels the Thessalonians with emphasis : " Never quench the fire of the
Spirit, never disdain prophetic revelations, but test them
all, retaining what is good." [1]   Paul was not unaware of the
dangers inherent in ecstatic worship, yet he seems never
to have wavered in his confidence that the Spirit's leading
was to be wholly trusted, and that it would be wrong to
seek ease and safety with some lesser but more calculable
guide.   And his faith was justified.   There was in this
Spirit-guided worship an ardour, a freshness, a variety,
a sincerity, and a creative power, that have sent their
pulse-beats throbbing through the worship of the centuries.
Because of their experience of the Spirit, these first worshippers felt within themselves that they had access to the
living sources of power.   They looked on others, plain
people like themselves, and beheld them suddenly made
possessors of hitherto unsuspected capacities and gifts.
On such a scale nothing like this had ever happened before.
A new age had dawned for the world, and they were its
heirs.   An even greater time was at hand when the Lord
himself would return to his own.   Meanwhile they waited,
well-content because the Spirit which He had sent was
among them, and was flooding their lives with peace and
love, giving them a new heart for their troubles and making
it a pure joy to come together for their worship, where
they would again experience this living power and be
drawn deeper into fellowship with one another and with
their Risen and Exalted Lord.

It is held by some, and not only by the more extreme
school of criticism, that, strictly speaking, " the idea of
the Spirit did not belong to the Gospel as proclaimed by
Jesus, and in some ways it brought an alien element into
his religion." [2]   In the message of Jesus, it is held, redemption meant essentially a renewal of the will, while the
doctrine of the Spirit introduced a different kind of power
co-operating with the moral forces released by the Gospel.

[1] I Thess. v. 19 ff.
[2] E. F. Scott, *The Spirit in the New Testament*, p. 245.

A discussion of this large question would lead too far afield. Still, the conditions at Corinth, so different from what we would conceive as likely to have sprung up under the personal control of Jesus, call at least for some elucidation of the practical issue of the ecstatic *versus* the moral.

One may well wonder what would have happened to the developing Religion if the excitements already showing at Corinth had been allowed to grow and spread. Quite conceivably the Corinthian assembly might have come to be something like a " mob of howling dervishes and Jump-to-glory-Janes." It was partly to avert such risks that Paul wrote those *Corinthian* chapters which are so invaluable for the study of the worship. He makes his appeal, first and foremost, to the instincts of fellowship. He will have everything discouraged which is unintelligible, and therefore unhelpful to the building up of a worshipping community. Not that he questioned the genuine inspiration of the *tongues* or of the ecstatic prophecies ; some were spurious, but in the main he believed them to be authentic fruits of the Spirit. Still, since the chief aim should be " edification," he pleads most earnestly for a recognition of the less showy and exciting of the gifts as being the most serviceable of all. However, it is in one aphoristic pronouncement that Paul discloses what is the heart and mainspring of his own thinking on the matter. " The spirits of the prophets are subject to the prophets." [1] In these words the Apostle's moral personality flashes out. He throws down a direct challenge to the notion, commonly entertained by the ecstatic himself, that he is in the grip of a power he cannot resist and must perforce yield to. Paul will not grant this even to the speaker with tongues : it is always in his power to " keep silent " if he will.[2] Still less will he grant it to the prophet, who, in his view, stands on a higher level than the speaker with tongues. The prophet's will remains at his disposal and is never beyond his control. *The spirits of the prophets are subject to the prophets.* Surely this is the voice of moral sanity ;

[1] I Cor. xiv. 32.　　　　[2] I Cor. xiv. 28.

or, to put it more fittingly, the voice of one whose mind and heart were steeped in fellowship with the personality of the Lord Jesus.

We can hardly overestimate the service rendered to the growing Religion by such affirmations of the superior value, in their own right, of her moral elements. The Church has not failed to do justice to Paul as the man of bold pioneering mind who greatly widened the horizons of her thought. Yet we must feel that he rendered an even more vital service when he gave his strength to head her off, in the days of her unchastened youth, from the perils of emotionalism and orgiasm. And when, as at Corinth and elsewhere, we find Paul wrestling with some dark and crucial problem and then suddenly turning upon it the flashlight of some great moral principle which illuminates it once and for all, it becomes difficult to understand those historians who accuse Paul, of all men, of being the arch-betrayer of his Faith and its worship to the seductions of Oriental mystery.

But great as were the services of Paul to the developing Worship, it was under stronger guardianship than his. The power of Christ himself was always upon it, to guide and control. This power was operative (1) in the Spirit-manifestations, and above all (2) in the celebration of the Lord's Supper.

(1) The Spirit was never conceived as a magnitude wholly separate from Christ. From the first they appear to have been closely connected. In the Old Testament the gift of the Spirit is associated with the promise of the Messiah ; while in the New Testament the Spirit is represented as the gift of the Risen Christ, sent to support his people.[1] Further, we cannot be wrong in thinking that while the Master was with his disciples on earth, they had been aware of something more in his message than a body of new truths and principles. There was Power, some quickening and constraining power that laid hold of them, however vaguely they may have defined it to themselves.

[1] E. F. Scott, *The Spirit in the New Testament*, p. 86.

Accordingly, when the Spirit came upon them after his death, it did not come as something wholly strange, and unrelated to him. On this ground alone we might feel confident that, from the first, their conception of the Spirit was baptized into Christ. Further, it is very possibly true, as has been maintained,[1] that it was while they were engaged in witnessing to the Resurrection that the Spirit first came upon them. They had been conscious of a prophetic constraint laid on them to witness of what they had seen, and even as they were witnessing they suddenly became aware of a new power that gave added fire to their hearts and words. If this be a true interpretation of their Pentecost experience, it provides another link in the connection of the Spirit with Christ. The further development of this connection we cannot trace with clearness until, some twenty years later, we find Paul writing in terms which go far towards equating the Spirit with Christ. It is not merely that in one passage he seems to identify them : " The Lord is that Spirit." [2] Still more significant is his equating of them for practical purposes, by assigning to them the same functions.[3] Most significant of all is the fact that while he regards the Spirit as the quickening power behind his whole Christian thinking and living, he at the same time regards Christ as the sphere in which he lives and moves. While it is certain that Paul's own vivid experience of Christ was responsible for hastening and maturing this development of thought, there is no evidence that he altogether outstripped the general thought of the Church and left it behind. We may conclude, therefore, that when the worshipper found himself under the sway of the Spirit, he believed that the power that swayed him was somehow the power of Christ, or at least a power closely associated with Him.

(2) It was in the celebration of the Lord's Supper that

[1] Karl Holl, *Gesammelte Aufsaetze zur Kirchengeschichte*, ii. 26.
[2] 2 Cor. iii. 17.
[3] Specially clear in Rom. viii. 9–11.

the consciousness of being under the hand of Christ reached its climax. The manner of this celebration is reserved for later treatment. Meantime, two more general facts are to be emphasised.

(a) The Lord's Supper brought the worshippers into the presence of their Risen and Exalted Lord. " Where two or three are gathered together in my name, there am I in the midst of them." [1] Whether or not these be authentic words of Jesus, they voice the belief of the worshipping Church. This simple belief that He was still living and present with them was one of the supremely creative factors in the growth and worship of the Church. He lived still ; was present at his own table in fellowship with his own people—a fellowship which some few of them had enjoyed at other meals which they had shared with him on earth. In what precise way his presence was realised we do not know. That it was a presence somehow localised in the bread and wine we cannot believe. That it was a presence conceived in some such fashion as they conceived the presence of the Spirit we may be confident. Perhaps a presence that enveloped and enswathed them like an atmosphere [2]—but we do not know. As they had learnt to construe their conception of the Spirit in terms of Christ, it is probable that they had also learnt to construe their conception of the presence of Christ in terms of the Spirit. For the rest, we must be content with this fact that they believed Him to be living, and present with them at their worship.

(b) The Lord's Supper focused their thoughts primarily upon the *death of Jesus*. We may feel certain that this celebration was the climax-point of their worship ; and the fact that in this supreme act of their fellowship their thoughts were anchored to the Jesus of history is a fact of the utmost significance. We are not here concerned with the speculations of Paul and of later thinkers on the profounder meanings of the Death. It is doubtful if

[1] Matt. xviii. 20.
[2] Cf. Deissmann, *St. Paul*, p. 128.

these speculations have played any prominent rôle in the vital communion-thoughts of the average worshipper in any age ; it is well-nigh certain that they played no such rôle in the spring-time of the worship. What gripped and held the earliest worshippers was the simple fact that when they sat at the Supper they had fellowship with a Risen and Exalted Lord who, within recent memory, had died as a real man dying a real death. This was the significant fact for that age—it was a *real* death and resurrection, not a mythical one. To realise the presence of a risen and exalted Lord was one thing—initiates of the Mysteries were doing that every day. To realise the presence of a risen and exalted Lord who carried the imprint of wounds inflicted on a certain day outside Jerusalem was a quite different thing. In the first place, such an One could not fail to draw the worshipper with " the cords of a man and the bands of love." " He loved me ; He gave himself for me." In the second place, such an One would discourage his believing people from following the fashion of the day and clothing their " Lord " with the imaginations of myth ; while, on the other hand, He strongly encouraged them to clothe his exalted Figure with the attributes which had been his during his life on earth. And if the moral ideal of our religion was firmly wrought into the texture of the Church's thought and life during this creative and plastic period, so firmly that it has never been displaced but has remained almost the one constant and abiding element through all the changes of the centuries, then we owe this result in no small degree to the twin facts, that, embedded in the centre of her teaching (and later in the centre of her sacred book) was the story of the life and death of Jesus, and that, enshrined at the heart of her daily or weekly worship was a solemn celebration which directed thought and devotion to the Jesus who died on a cross and whose death was the epitome and consummation of the spirit of his life.

To sum up. Their Worship-communion was with God through One who was at once Spirit, Indwelling Christ,

Exalted Lord, and the Lord Jesus of history.   But, thanks to the *Gospels* and the Lord's Supper, it was with the last-named of these, the Lord Jesus of history, that the final and controlling word continued to rest.[1]

[1] See the closing pages of this book.

CHAPTER IV

The Worship in its Joyous Confidence

SINCE it was in Worship that the Religion found its
fullest expression, we may be sure that the note of
Joy, so evident in its literature, rang out even more clearly
in its worship-assemblies. One has read somewhere
of a journalist whose day's work took him to a conference
of Salvation Army officers and workers, and who said
afterwards that he had never, in his wide experience of
public gatherings, seen such a crowd of happy faces. In
the worship of the early Church there were richer and
grander notes sounded than would be the case at that
conference ; but its irrepressible Joy was true to the great
tradition.

It is not our task to lay bare the sources of this Joy ;
to do so were to unfold the unsearchable riches which
already the Church had discovered in Christ. Her joy
was the joy of Redemption : of emancipation from the
servitude of Sin, from the bondage of the Law, from the
tyranny of Death, from the dominion of Satan and his
hordes of sinister spirits. It was the joy of Hope—the
thrilling hope of the Parousia, the coming-again of Christ.
It was the joy of Forgiveness and Reconciliation with God ;
of Fellowship with Him through the Spirit ; of Fellowship
with Christ, and with one another through Christ. Very
clearly the note of joy is rung out in the early chapters
of *Acts*. The disciples as they ate " with a glad and
simple heart praising God," were no children of gloom.
Nor were the Apostles with their " boldness of speech,"
giving their testimony to the resurrection of Jesus " with
great power " ; nor Stephen, whose face " shone like the
face of an angel." And the note of joy goes ringing

through the whole literature. Behind Paul's epistles we discern people with happy faces ; from the Thessalonians, who welcomed the word, though it brought them heavy trouble, " with a joy inspired by the Holy Spirit," right on to the Philippians, bidden to " rejoice in the Lord, and again I say, rejoice." Even James, a drier type of man, knows of a " pure joy " which comes in the wake of trials ; while the authors of the Apocalypse and the First Epistle of John write triumphantly of " the victory that has overcome the world."

> " The man who has shared this basal experience of victorious joy and confidence, he—and only he— can understand Primitive Christianity." [1]

But though we do not here attempt to unfold the rich content of the New Testament Joy, we must try to recapture some of the tones and colours of its expression in worship.

In the absence of direct evidence as to the prevailing atmospheres of the early worship, we may safely assume that they were substantially one with the atmospheres pervading the literature. When, for instance, we learn from Paul's letters that his own life of fellowship with God was habitually keyed to certain notes, we may conclude that these same notes were struck in the worship of the community. For Paul's spiritual life had been nurtured within the worshipping Church, and his commanding personality, in its turn, had been steadily reacting upon the Church, leading it into deeper regions of experience and thought. Accordingly, far though he may have surpassed others in force and range of mind, we may feel sure that in the united outpouring of hearts before God he and they were at one.

A case in point will serve to open up our subject. When Paul gives expression to his feelings towards God and Christ, he is markedly sparing in the use of the language of " love." It is not Paul who calls Christ his " beloved " ;

[1] J. Weiss, *Urchristentum*, p. 29.

nor does he ever write in the strain of what we call
" emotionalism " ; in only five places,[1] in all his letters,
does he speak expressly of love as directed towards God or
Christ. And this reserve in the use of such love-language
is characteristic of the New Testament. " From the
first, love in Christianity was an affection rather than an
emotion " ; [2] it involved mind and will as well as heart ;
a love dissociated from duty and reflection would not be
true Christian love. We conclude, therefore, that the
early worship was not hospitable to emotionalism. No
doubt there were outbreaks of it, but it could not long
flourish in the prevailing atmosphere. In contrast with
the Mystery faiths, which offered to their worshippers, as
proofs of the divine favour, a number of sensations and
emotions, Christianity did not seek for assurance of her
faith from among the movements of her own subjective
feelings. Though her assurance was rooted in experience,
it rested ultimately on objective things—things which had
been seen with the eye or heard with the ear: the great
things which God had done in Christ, and the great things
He still was doing through the Spirit. It was upon these
that the gaze of the worshipper was steadily turned.

And so his joy was no shallow or effervescent thing. It
was a joy that was always touched with awe, and kept
sober by this habit of adoring contemplation. The
historical character of the Jewish and the Christian
religions was nowhere more clearly disclosed than in their
prayers at public worship. Sometimes a whole chain of
historical events would be made the object of the prayer-
contemplation ; or some single event, such as the death
and resurrection of Christ ; or His single saving personality
—but always it was something pertaining to the realm of
historical fact that was the motive of thanksgiving and
praise. As we shall see later, neither confession nor
petition (as distinct from intercession) bulked large in the
content of the early prayers ; glad and adoring praise

---

[1] Moffatt, *Love in the New Testament*, 154 ff.

[2] Moffatt, *op. cit.* p. 55.

was their pre-eminent theme. " Rejoice at all times ;
never give up prayer ; thank God for everything—such is
his will for you in Jesus Christ." [1]

It needs no great perspicacity to discern behind such
phrases as these an unusual warmth and gladness ; for
though " emotionalism " was eschewed, there was no ban
laid upon the nobler of the primal feelings that lie deep
in the heart of man the world over. Thus we find the
family-feelings coming to their own in Christian worship
in a way they had not done even in Judaism. " Father "
and " Brothers " were two of the words most frequent on
the lips of worshippers. Another significant pointer
to this " ultimate humanism " of the worship is to be seen
in the term which the young religion adopted to designate
its prayers of praise and thanks to God. *Eucharistein*—
to give thanks—became the favourite word. Now the
favourite word in the Jewish worship was represented by
eulogein—to praise, or bless—and while the Jewish word
is suggestive of the homage paid by a subject to his king,
the Christian word is charged with the simpler but deeper
feelings of grateful love which a child cherishes towards
his father. One scholar has shown in detail how marked
is the New Testament preference for the warmer and more
intimately personal *eucharistein*, and he concludes : [2]

> " This marked predominance of the word in the New
> Testament cannot be an accident, when we consider
> that this word was not only frequent on the lips of
> Jesus, and used in almost every one of Paul's letters,
> but is rarely to be found in the old Jewish prayers,
> and never in their opening formulæ. The Jewish
> piety confined itself, for the most part, to reverential
> praise of the Almighty, and its thanksgiving took the
> form of homage. It was only when it came into
> touch with the spirit of Jesus Christ that it learned
> to thank the holy God as a child thanks its father,

[1] 1 Thess. v. 17 f.
[2] Von der Goltz, *Das Gebet in der aeltesten Christenheit*, p. 105.

3

and so brought to the front the word which rang with this personal note. Prayer became personal prayer of thanksgiving, where previously it had been rather an ascription of praise."

This is one of the reasons why, with Paul and John, the idea of the Kingdom of God recedes into the background, in favour of the warmer conception of the Family of God. Christians habitually addressed each other as *brothers*. True, the term was in common use among the members of the Pagan guilds and cannot be claimed as distinctively Christian ; but it echoed a great thought of Jesus : " Whosoever doeth the will of God, the same is my brother and sister and mother," and it gave fitting expression to the intimate family-feeling that pervaded the early fellowships. The *holy kiss* was a symbolic action, expressive of the same feeling. It was exchanged either during, or at the commencement of worship ; and the custom rooted itself so deeply that Tertullian, at the end of the second century, could say that no prayer was complete apart from the kiss that followed it. As the churches grew in number, abuses crept in and the practice had to be restricted, men now kissing men and women women. But in the earliest period the kiss of " peace," or of " love," remained a simple and spontaneous expression of the warm family-feeling which prevailed amongst the worshippers.[1]

If the kiss of peace was the most demonstrative expression of their glad sense of fellowship, a deeper expression was reached through the medium of a metaphor that came to be a prime favourite with Paul. The *Body of Christ* he calls the Christian worshippers.[2] The metaphor is frequent in literary Greek, in phrases like our " body-politic " ; and quite possibly Paul got it from that source. He employs it frequently, analysing and applying it in a variety of ways, and discovering so remarkable a correspondence between the human body and the fellowship it was used to illustrate, that in the end it ceases to be a mere

[1] Cf. Moffatt, *op. cit.* 246.　　　　[2] I Cor. xii. 27.

metaphor and becomes something more. What began as a comparison ends in being a symbol which goes some way towards becoming an identification : " Ye *are* the Body of Christ." The metaphor is certainly an extraordinarily apt one, as descriptive of the functioning of a Worship-assembly under the control of the Spirit.[1] Members rising to their feet, one after another, each performing his separate function in the complete act of worship, and all alike controlled by the one animating Power—it is hard to avoid the surmise that it must have been on some occasion when Paul sat at worship observing all this that its likeness to a human body, moving harmoniously in obedience to its central control, flashed for the first time into his mind. Bousset maintains that " when Paul speaks of the Christian community as a Body of which the Head is Christ, always he is visualising the community as gathered together for worship." [2] This conception of the Church as the Body of Christ was to prove a most creative and fruitful one ; but our present concern is to observe how close was the fellowship as thus conceived. It was fellowship at once with Christ the Head and with each other as co-operating members of his divine Body. The Body of Christ ! Each worshipper an actual member of that living Body ! As they began to realise what this meant, we can well conceive their joy growing deeper and more devout ; while already some few would draw their spirits apart, into mystic contemplation of this wondrous fellowship into which they had been called by God. In John's image of the Vine we find a " peculiarly perfect image," as Heiler calls it, of this intimate union and fellowship. Nowadays, he adds, we are apt to interpret it too abstractly ; whereas, if we look at it, not in isolation, but against the background of Christian worship, it acquires new life, and we discern something of the " glory of the Christ-mysticism which was associated with that worship." [3]

Although this conception of the Church as the Body of

[1] Rom. xii. 5-8.   [2] *Kyrios Christos*[1], p. 105.
[3] *The Spirit of Worship*, p. 24 f.

Christ needed little help from other conceptions to give it depth and fervour, it was greatly widened in its range, as indeed all Christian thought was widened, by another conception, namely that of the Church as *the Ecclesia of God*. It will suffice here to set down what is now generally thought to have been the content of this conception, without touching on questions of the origin and order of emergence of its various elements.

(*a*) The Church, as composed of its worshipping assemblies, was conceived as essentially one. The Corinthian assembly was not merely the " church of Corinth " ; it was " the Church of God at Corinth," that part of the great living organism functioning at Corinth. Parallel with this designation of individual churches as belonging to the one Church of God was the designation of individual worshippers as " saints," people called by God and set apart for special privilege and service.

(*b*) The term *Ecclesia*—Church—gave expression to the deep consciousness that the Church represented the true Israel of God, and was heir to Israel's promises and privileges, and in particular had inherited its task of bringing blessing to the whole world. This exalted consciousness reveals itself in quite an incidental way—showing how familiar it had already become—when Paul writes : " Put no stumbling-block in the way of Jews, or Greeks, or the Church of God," as though the Church of God were a third race of men, alongside of Jews and Greeks. The Church was the *People* of God.

(*c*) The Church became the heir not only to a great past but also to the promise and certainty of a still greater future. She was the *People*, chosen anew by God, to share with Him the glories of the coming Kingdom, when the old order would be swept away, and Christ would take his place as Lord of all, and they would reign with Him.

This sketch of the main content of the *Ecclesia* conception may suffice to suggest how greatly it must have exalted the mood of the worshipper, giving to his joy at once a wider range and a surer confidence. It is a mistake, surely, to think of the Church as beginning her career with only meagre ambitions, and with horizons commensurate with the narrow and restricted circumstances of her origin. Nor is it conceivable that she started on her course with no clear sense of direction, and only afterwards, by some sort of accident, stumbled on her vocation. There is really no good ground for hesitating to believe that from her earliest days she possessed at least the substance of the great thoughts we have been sketching, and that her worshippers could have responded to the impassioned words of a later teacher :

> " Ye are a chosen generation, a royal priesthood, an holy nation, a peculiar people : that ye should show forth the praises of him who hath called you out of darkness into his marvellous light : which in times past were not a people, but now are the People of God." [1]

Happily we can detect a few clear traces of the presence of these exalted notes in the early worship.

(1) It is widely agreed that one of the sayings of Jesus at the Last Supper that can be most confidently retained as authentic is his assertion that he would not drink henceforth of the fruit of the vine until that day when he would drink it *new* with his disciples in his Father's Kingdom. The Messianic Banquet had become established in apocalyptic imagery. It was congenial to the thought of the time as descriptive of " joyous fellowship and the satisfaction of all desires." [2] It depicted a perpetual feast of gladness, prepared for the Messiah's people in the Kingdom of God, at which He would himself preside. So when his disciples, after his death, continued their fellowship with Him round their Supper-table, we may be sure that frequently they felt themselves to be lifted above space and time, and to be enjoying a foretaste of this heavenly Feast of joy. " Eye hath not seen, nor ear heard,

---

[1] 1 Pet. ii. 9 f.
[2] Scott, *The Kingdom and the Messiah*, p. 241.

neither have entered into the heart of man, the things which God hath prepared for them that love him." [1] This old prophetic thought, already taken over by Paul, soon gained for itself a place in the worship of the Church. It appears in *1 Clement*, in association with the *Sanctus*, and in subsequent Liturgies it has an established position. For it gave worthy expression to the worshippers' glad sense of wonder at the greatness of the future that lay in front, foretastes of which they were enjoying even now as they gathered in Christ's name at his own Table.

(2) We have evidence that the *Sanctus* had established a place for itself in the worship of the New Testament Church. The writer of *1 Clement* was already familiar, about the turn of the century, with the sound of the *Holy, Holy, Holy*, as it ascended from the voices of assembled worshippers.[2] From *Hebrews* with its conception of religion as synonymous with worship, and from the majestic pictures of the heavenly worship in the *Apocalypse of John* we infer that, very early, there had emerged the thought that the Church's worship was the antitype of a more glorious worship above, and that the strains of both were blended together as they rose to the throne of God. In *Revelation* v. 11–14, we find an antiphony of praise to Christ, between *the many angels round about the throne and the beasts and the elders* on the one hand and, on the other, *every creature which is in heaven—* such as stars and birds—*and on the earth, and such as are in the sea.* First the praise from heaven ascends ; then the praise from earth ; and the final response to the earthly praise is given in the heavenly *Amen.* This must surely be an echo of antiphonal praises to Christ which the writer had heard in his own familiar Worship ; such praises as Pliny [3] was to report to his Emperor as being an established feature of Christian worship in the early years of the second century.

[1] 1 Cor. ii. 9.
[2] *1 Clem.* 34.
[3] " Carmen Christo quasi Deo dicere *secum invicem.*"—Ep. x. 96.

" The local community, when in public worship it prays and sings praises, knows itself to be one with the choir of angels who surround the throne of God and without ceasing chant the *Holy, Holy, Holy* ; one with the brethren who have been made perfect, whom the author of the *Apocalypse* beheld standing before the throne of the Lamb clothed in white robes, offering prayer and intercession.   The Church militant forms with the Church triumphant one great community of prayer ; nay, this Church of Christ extends throughout the whole universe, the mighty choirs of which glorify the eternal Father through Jesus Christ, with one mind and with one voice." [1]

The earliest Church, though she worshipped in very humble meeting-places, reached out her arms towards a fellowship that was world-wide and heaven-high ; and the joy of her worship on earth was attuned to the majestical Joy of the worship above.

[1] Heiler, *The Spirit of Worship*, p. 23.

CHAPTER V

THE WORSHIP AS SPIRIT-CONTROLLED

A. ENTHUSIASM

CHRISTIAN WORSHIP, during its classic period which lasted till after the death of Paul, was enthusiastic, in the full religious sense of the word: it was God-inspired, Spirit-filled. This was its character from the earliest days. We do not begin to understand it till we realise that belief in the Spirit as the dominant operative influence in worship was cardinal.

The Church's belief in the Spirit sprang from her experience of a fact.[1] Very early in her career—probably at Pentecost—the disciples became aware of a new power working within them. Its most striking manifestation at first was *glossolalia*, " speaking with tongues," a power of ecstatic utterance in unintelligible speech ; and both those seized by this power and those who saw and heard its manifestations were convinced that some Power from a higher world had broken into their lives, endowing them with capacities of utterance and with other gifts, which appeared to be something quite different from a mere heightening of endowments already theirs. People who hitherto had seemed to be nothing out of the common suddenly became capable of impassioned prayer and speech, or of lofty moods in which they were manifestly holding converse with the Unseen. *Acts* records many

---

[1] " It cannot be too often repeated that belief in the Spirit has always arisen out of actual experience, and that the Primitive Church did not arrive at it by brooding over ancient texts and precedents. The belief was the expression of a fact." (E. F. Scott, *The Spirit in the New Testament*, p. 61.)

forms of the manifestations—speaking with tongues :
moving eloquence : [1] vision of the unseen : [2] prophetic
insight : [3] knowledge of men's thoughts and words.[4] *Paul*
extends the list of manifestations. The special gifts
of Apostles, Prophets, Teachers, are attributed to the
Spirit ; also gifts of service and administration — in
short, every marked capacity evinced in the worship, or in
the service of the cause, seems to have been credited to
the Spirit. And always it was conceived, in Old Testament fashion, as a new and foreign power descending upon
men from God. At first, it was thought to be an inter-
mittent visitant that comes and goes and returns again.
Later, it was conceived as the more or less permanent
possession of every Christian, though its presence might
be more evident at some times than at others. Finally,
by Paul, it was regarded as a power permeating and
recreating the whole Christian life, the abiding source and
inspiration of all Christian thought and feeling and action,
and yet, none the less, a Power from on high.

As to the meaning put upon these experiences by the
first Christians, the material for interpreting them lay
ready to hand in their Scriptures. The Spirit of God,
they said, had come upon them, even as it came upon the
saints and prophets of old : nay, it had been foretold by
the prophets themselves, when they said that the Spirit
would be poured out in larger measure in the last days. It
is quite unnecessary, therefore, to seek explanations from
Hellenistic sources either of the experiences or of their
interpretation. The evidence points to the belief in the
Spirit having been established before ever the Church
moved out into the Hellenistic world." [5]

---

[1] iv. 8 ; vi. 5.   [2] Acts vii. 55.
[3] xi. 28.   [4] viii. 29 ; xi. 12.

[5] If the reliability of *Acts* as a witness be called in question, it is
to be noted that both the *Apocalypse of John* and the *Epistle to the
Hebrews* (ii. 4) are in accord with the Old Testament ideas of a
power which suddenly irrupts into the lives of men ; and neither of

It will elucidate matters if, at this point, we come to terms of understanding with the strange phenomenon of *speaking with tongues*, which appears to have been the most arresting and at first the most characteristic of the manifestations of the Spirit. It will suffice to summarise the results of such studies as those of Kirsopp Lake,[1] E. F. Scott,[2] and J. Weiss.[3]

(1) The original meaning of " to speak with tongues " was probably not " to speak in a foreign language," but " to speak in *another* language "—the language of heaven, which, though unintelligible to men, was intelligible to God : cf. " tongues of men and of angels." The other meaning lay close at hand, and may have been the popular one as it has been in some modern revivals.

(2) The phenomenon was not peculiar to early Christianity. There were pagan parallels : the Delphian prophetess ; the magic papyri. There have been more recent manifestations : Montanists ; Camisards ; Irvingites ; Methodists ; American revivals. Modern psychology accounts for the phenomenon as due to the overwhelming strain and stress of religious emotion, seeking for an outlet and striving to express the thoughts at its heart. This explanation will probably stand ; but it is to be noted that, while it may explain the immediate cause, it does not profess to account for the ultimate cause, which lay in the overwhelming emotion. It still remains to

these books bears any trace, at this point, of the mystical conceptions of Hellenism. Also, the early chapters of the *Gospel of Luke*, which must have been written under Palestinian influence, describe the Spirit as descending upon Zechariah, Elizabeth, and Simeon, in the manner of a power which comes down upon men from God, impelling them to marvellous speech, or to inspired knowledge of the unseen. The witness of *Acts* does not stand alone.

[1] *Earlier Epistles of Paul*, pp. 241–252.
[2] *The Spirit in the New Testament*, chap. iv.
[3] *Commentary on 1 Corinthians*, excursus on xiv. 26.

discover any better explanation of that emotion than was given by the Church when she attributed it to the Spirit of God.

(3) At Corinth the gift was highly prized, to the depreciation of other gifts. In dealing with its excesses, Paul shows his great sanity of judgment, and his instinctive adherence to the moral ideal as finally determinative. He has never a doubt as to *speaking with tongues* being a genuine gift of the Spirit ; he possesses the gift himself ; [1] possibly the " sighs which are beyond words " [2] are an echo from his own prayer experience, when speech proved inadequate to express what he would utter to God. We return later to Paul's method of dealing with the matter.

(4) Perhaps the prevalence of *speaking with tongues* at Corinth was not typical of the Church generally. Thessalonica appears to have been less hospitable to the manifestations.[3] If there was ever real danger of Christianity becoming an orgiastic religion, it was averted by the superior strength of the moral forces released by the Gospel. As the century advanced and the enthusiasm cooled, the phenomenon would be less and less in evidence, yielding finally before the growing pressure of church-order and organisation.

How deeply the Spirit was rooted in the Church's belief and worship is shown by a multiplicity of references in the New Testament, of which a few of the more significant may be cited. Paul makes possession of the Spirit to be the test of the reality of a man's religion. " If any man have not the Spirit of Christ, he is none of his." [4] He asks the Galatians whether it was by the works of the law or by the hearing of faith that they had received the Spirit, " as if the reception of the Spirit was something as definite and observable as, for example, an attack of influenza." [5] In Paul's thought and in John's the Spirit was so firmly

[1] 1 Cor. xiv. 6, 18.   [2] Rom. viii. 26.   [3] 1 Thess. v. 19.
[4] Rom. viii. 9.   [5] Streeter, *The Primitive Church*, p. 69.

established that neither of them makes any endeavour to part with it, although their idea of Christ as Indwelling and as Logos had drawn into His hands practically all the functions of the Spirit and left no real need for the old conception. Further, the developed vocabulary, descriptive of the Spirit's operations, is noteworthy. Paul speaks of them in a threefold aspect. They are *charismata*, or a variety of gifts bestowed by the one Spirit : *diakoniai*, or varieties of service rendered to the cause of the one Lord : and *energemata*, or varieties of the dynamic effects of the power of the one God who works all in all. These three words [1] disclose a sweep of developed thought which must have been the result of much experience and reflection. All that was felt, and said, and done within the worship-assemblies was believed to be under the Spirit's control. When the perplexed sinner was filled with a quite new feeling of trust so that he cried, " Abba, Father," what was that but the Spirit bearing witness that he now belonged to the family of God ? [2] " God's love floods our hearts "— actually and palpably—" through the Holy Spirit which has been given to us." [3] Even the humble-seeming aptitudes for ministration to the needy are attributed to the same Power.[4]

We moderns may wonder why the Church did not recognise the majority of these endowments to be just natural gifts and capacities, quickened and heightened by the power of Christ, and why she did not seek an explanation of the more arresting endowments along the same line. Yet the fact remains that precisely the opposite view was taken. The more marvellous gifts controlled the interpretation of all, and drew every phenomenon of the worship within the sphere of the Spirit. In this we find an index of the extent to which the early Church was dominated by the conviction that the living power of God was abroad in her midst. As that Power had burst anew into human history in Jesus, and through concrete action

---

[1] 1 Cor. xii. 4–6.   [2] Rom. viii. 16.
[3] v. 5.   [4] 1 Cor. xii. 28.

in his life and death had wrought out redemption for men,
so it continued still to break into men's lives, dowering
them with power from on high. Not only was the basis
of their salvation objective ; the process of its completion,
through experiences such as those that met them in
worship, was in a real sense objective also. It was the
work of a Power that came upon them with palpable
manifestation. As day by day, in their worship-assemblies,
they beheld now one man, now another, swept to his feet
and impelled to unwonted speech and action, their minds
acquired a certain habit of objective poise. What was
happening in their worship was not of their own doing,
but of God's. " Not unto us, O Lord, not unto us, but
unto thy name be the glory." Their gaze had little
occasion to turn inward upon themselves ; mainly it was
directed outwards, in adoring contemplation of the wondrous
things which God had done for them in Christ, and still
was doing for them through His Spirit. We shall have
frequent occasion to return to this important aspect of
the worship. Meantime we observe that in this objective
habit of mind we have an explanation of the massive
simplicity and the glow of wholesome emotion, restrained
and reverential, which so signally distinguish many of
the great prayers in the earlier Liturgies of the Church.

The flame of Enthusiasm, ever kindled anew by the deeds
of the Spirit, was fed from another contributory source.
Apocalyptic Hopes burned in their hearts. Perhaps the
oldest legacy that we possess from the Church's worship
is the word *Maranatha*. It appears in 1 Cor. xvi. 22, and
in the *Didachê*, chap. x., and without doubt lies behind
the " Come, Lord Jesus " of Rev. xxii. 20. In the two
New Testament places it appears in the closing sentences
of a book ; while in the *Didachê* it forms the close of an
act of worship. The word is really composed of two
Aramaic words, which admit of being translated in either
of two ways : " The Lord comes," or " Come, Lord."
The latter is probably the meaning in our documents. In

any case, the position of these words at the close of the
Didachê formulary of worship, and their position in near
proximity to the benediction [1] in the two New Testament
writings strongly suggest that they formed part of the
customary closing act of Christian worship in the earliest
days. If that be so, then it was upon the apocalyptic
note that the worship ended. Eagerly the minds of
worshippers were strained forward in expectation of the
day, which they confidently believed to be near, when
their Lord himself would return to his people to consummate
his Kingdom. More than that—they believed the Kingdom
to be already in being; the decisive step had been taken;
the new age had begun. The community of believing
worshippers was "like a fragment of the future order
projected into the present; an outpost of the kingdom
thrust out into this world of time." [2] Its potencies were
even now at work in their assemblies: they were already
"tasting the powers of the world to come." [3] But when
the great expected day arrived, then they would behold
their Lord coming in his glory to end this present age
with its imperfections and evils; to subdue the banded
powers of Satan; to take his place as Lord of all. For it
was no mere drama of individual salvation that was to
be consummated then; nor even a drama on some national
scale. It was a drama involving the destinies of the
whole world, nay, of the whole created cosmos of God.
It may be difficult for us to think ourselves back into that

---

[1] It is worth noting that in the *Apocalypse of John*, and in several
of the *Letters of Paul*, the writer's instinct seems to be to begin and
close his writing on the note of worship, as though he sought to set
his work within the framework of an act of worship. Lohmeyer in
particular emphasises this in his Commentaries on the *Apocalypse*
and on *Colossians* (see on *Apoc.* xxii. 17–20; *Col.* Intro. sec. iii.).
Perhaps the immediate motive came from the writer's knowledge
that his work would be read by some church, gathered for worship.
In any case it is an indication of the prominent rôle which worship
played, that it was able thus to draw within its orbit even the
author as he bent over his task.

[2] E. F. Scott.   [3] Heb. vi. 5.

old world of apocalyptic thought ; but even a slight acquaintance with it enables us to sense the fervid expectancy that throbbed in its denizens, quickening their joyous hope, stretching out their minds, and fanning their Enthusiasm to a warmer glow.

B. FREEDOM.

Paul has been called the apostle of Liberty, and few would deny his claim to the title ; yet he was only formulating and working out a principle which was to be found already in full operation in every Christian Worship-assembly he entered. *" Where the Spirit of the Lord is, there is Liberty."* These words might have stood over the doorway of the most humble of the meeting-places of the early Church, as an appropriate motto. From the first, the control of the Spirit was taken seriously. The impressions we gather from reading the twelfth to the fourteenth chapters of *1 Corinthians* are consonant only with a worship where the Spirit's guidance was accepted as final, and where no lesser control was recognised. We shall not therefore expect to find many fixed and settled forms of worship in the early Church, but, rather, much diversity and freedom.

First, however, we consider a more general matter.

A great deal of our modern controversy about the government and worship of the early Church has been vitiated by failure to recognise this fundamental quality of Liberty in the early religion. Later churches and sects have each sought in the New Testament for the prototype of its own constitution and worship. Streeter writes pointedly on this matter.

> " The Episcopalian has sought to find episcopacy, the Presbyterian presbyterianism, and the Independent a system of independency to be the form of Church government in New Testament times. But while each party to the dispute has been able to make out

a case for his own view, he has never succeeded in demolishing the case of his opponent. The explanation of this deadlock, I have come to believe, is quite simple. It is the uncriticised assumption, made by all parties to the controversy, that in the first century there existed a single type of Church order." [1]

Streeter's main thesis is that " there is no basis in history for the traditional picture of the Apostles sitting together, like a College of Cardinals, systematising the doctrine and superintending the organisation of the Church." [2] " The actual course of events was of a more haphazard, and at the same time, of a more dynamic character—an original diversity, a rapid evolution in response to urgent local needs, to be followed later by standardisation up to an efficient uniform model." [3] " The history of Catholic Christianity during the first five centuries is the history of a progressive standardisation of a diversity which had its origin in the Apostolic age." [4] At the end of his inquiry, Streeter summarises thus :

" There is one result from which there is no escape. In the Primitive Church there was no single system of Church Order laid down by the Apostles. During the first hundred years of Christianity, the Church was an organism alive and growing, changing its organisation to meet changing needs. Clearly in Asia, Syria, and Rome during that century the system of government varied from church to church, and in the same church at different times. Uniformity was a later development ; and for those times it was, perhaps, a necessary development." [5]

It is not within the province of our present inquiry to deal closely with this vexed question of Church Order and Government ; but when that field is surveyed from the angle of the Worship, a simple but important conclusion

[1] *The Primitive Church*, Introdn. viii.
[2] P. 27.   [3] P. 72.   [4] P. 47.   [5] P. 261.

appears to thrust itself forward. *The Church at this early time was, for all practical purposes, simply the sum of her Worship-assemblies ; and her affairs were " governed " by the Leaders of Worship*

(a) *The Worship-assemblies were the Church.* As a visible institution, she had nothing to show, nothing to administer, outside of these gatherings and the few simple matters that were administered from them. She possessed no buildings, no property that needed " management." There was as yet no organisation, strictly speaking, binding the different churches together. Certain bonds did unite them—customs of hospitality to passing Christian strangers ; Apostles and others visiting from church to church, exhorting, advising, guiding ; occasional collectings and dispatchings of money to needy churches and workers elsewhere ; and, over all, the invisible bond of the *Ecclesia* making them, ideally, one Church of God. But as yet there was no actual organisation, such as would call for men to be set apart to control it. As a visible institution, the Church and the sum of her Worship-assemblies were one and the same thing.

(b) *She was " governed " by her Leaders of Worship.* When there was need for an important decision on some question of administration, such as the selection of missionaries for a decisively new venture, how was the decision made ?

> " Now in the church at Antioch there were prophets and teachers, Barnabas, Simeon, and Lucius the Cyrenian, besides Manaen and Saul. As they were worshipping the Lord, and fasting, the Holy Spirit said : ' Come, set me apart Barnabas and Saul for the work to which I have called them.' Then after fasting and prayer they laid their hands on them and let them go." [1]

This means that the momentous decision was taken during an act of worship. It was believed that the issue

[1] Acts xiii. 1–3.

4

had already been determined by the Spirit ;[1] it remained only to discover, through worship, what the mind of the Spirit was ; and the men best equipped for this task were the men who had shown themselves most susceptible to the Spirit's leading—in this case, the Prophets and Teachers, who were the outstanding figures in the local worship. The inference seems inevitable. The great affairs of the Church were directed by the men who, as leaders in worship, possessed the freest access to the Presence-chamber of the supreme governing Will.

Now, Paul makes it abundantly clear who these men, in his day, were. They were the Apostles, Prophets, and Teachers. These were elevated above the others, not in virtue of any " office " to which they had been appointed— that seems clear from the *Corinthians* passage immediately to be quoted—but in virtue of their personal endowment by the Spirit. The Spirit had chosen them, above others, to be his mouthpieces ; daily they exercised their superior gift ; and automatically, it would seem, they passed, in virtue of it, into the order of *Apostle*, or of *Prophet*, or of *Teacher*, as the case might be.

Paul's earliest pronouncement is in 1 Cor. xii. 28 :

> " And God hath set some in the church, first apostles, secondly prophets, thirdly teachers, then miracles, then gifts of healings, helps, governments, divers kinds of tongues."—R.V.

Here, priority is assigned to Apostles, Prophets, and Teachers. The Apostles were a special class, with spheres of activity rarely, if ever, confined to one church or locality ; accordingly the Prophet and Teacher must represent " the two most important offices in what may be called the normal ministry in a local church."[2]   On the other hand,

---

[1] Cf. Acts xv. 28—" It seemed good to the Holy Spirit and to us."

[2] Streeter, *op. cit.* 77.   " The notion that a Prophet was usually a person who led a wandering life is an entirely mistaken deduction from the *Didaché* : the fact that some Prophets led that kind of life is no evidence that all or even that a majority did so." *Ibid.* 77.

" helps " and " governments " evidently point to persons
endowed with capacities of practical service and administration, rather than with gifts of utterance ; and these appear
far down in the list ; not even at the end, where some
importance might have been suggested, but second-last
and third-last, giving a suggestion of quite minor standing.

Next in order of time is the *Romans* passage (xii. 6–8) :

> " And having gifts differing according to the grace
> that was given to us, whether prophecy, let us prophesy
> according to the proportion of our faith ; or ministry,
> let us give ourselves to our ministry ; or he that
> teacheth, to his teaching ; or he that exhorteth, to his
> exhorting ; he that giveth, let him do it with liber-
> ality ; he that ruleth, with diligence ; he that showeth
> mercy, with cheerfulness."

Here again " he that ruleth " comes far down the list,
while the Prophet and Teacher still stand high up.   On the
other hand, " ministry " has received a marked advancement.   Possibly it corresponds to " helps " in the earlier
list, and seems to point to persons with functions akin to
the functions of the Deacons at Jerusalem, who *ministered*
to the needs of the poor.   It is to be noted that in both the
quoted passages this ministry to the needy takes precedence
of " governments " and " rule."

When we come to *Ephesians* [1] (iv. 11), the development
is more marked.

> " And he gave some to be apostles ; and some,
> prophets ; and some, evangelists ; and some, pastors
> and teachers."

Streeter maintains that the Pastors (" Shepherds " : in
the Old Testament equivalent to " Rulers ") are

[1] For those who cannot accept the Pauline authorship, the
Ephesian passage may still remain good evidence for the order of
things in some first-century Pauline church in Asia.   The close
affinities of *Ephesians* to *Colossians*, coupled with the fact of its
being known, apparently, to all of the Apostolic Fathers, point to
an early date, and to a destination somewhere in Asia Minor.

" obviously equivalent to *Episcopoi* (" Bishops ") ; but they are no longer nameless as in the Corinthian letter, but come between the Prophets and Teachers." [1] It is doubtful to what extent the designation " Bishop " had come into vogue at this early period ; but it seems clear, in any case, that the need for administrative rule, to secure coherence in the expanding Church, was now being clearly recognised—a need which Paul had already sensed in his earliest letter to the turbulent church at Corinth.[2] By the end of the century the movement is in full swing ; in the *Didachê*, and more markedly in the *Ignatian Letters*, the strengthening of the administrative element has become a central aim. But our concern here is rather with the *terminus a quo* ; and it seems clear that the initial order of things, as reflected specially in *Corinthians*, was one in which the Worship-assemblies held a dominant place in the life of the Church, and the men who led their worship were pre-eminent in the guidance of the Church's affairs— a position which they owed to their pre-eminent possession of the gifts of the Spirit.

We must now come closer to our immediate subject, which is the *Freedom of the Worship*. In a Church that turned for leadership not to men of system and ordered rule, but to men distinguished for their inspired thought and utterance, we should not expect fixed and settled forms of worship, uniform throughout the churches ; we should expect, rather, much diversity and freedom. And that is what we do find.

> " The student of Liturgiology will hardly need to be reminded that each of the great centres of Christianity evolved its own type of Liturgy. But attempts to trace these back to their earliest form suggest that, apart from a very few constant features, there existed a maximum of freedom and diversity in the earliest period." [3]

[1] *Op. cit.* 81.   [2] i Cor. xvi. 15 f.   [3] Streeter, *op. cit.* 52.

The *Lord's Supper* provides an example. The more closely we examine the details of the celebration during the New Testament period, the more impressed we are with the freedom and diversity disclosed. What could be more dissimilar than the Supper-conceptions of the *Didachê*, emanating from Syria, and the conceptions disclosed in the sixth chapter of John's Gospel, emanating almost contemporaneously from the region of Ephesus ? Or what unity of form could we hope to extract from the five Lord's Supper formularies which appear in *Matthew, Mark, Luke, 1 Cor.* xi., and the *Didachê*, to say nothing of the references in *Acts* to the Breaking of Bread ? Incessant effort has been spent during the centuries to reconcile these formularies with each other and with the presupposition that they have all come into being as copies of a single original model set up by Jesus at the Last Supper in Jerusalem. Through very despair of the hope of reconciliation, some scholars in the more recent past have surmised that the old presupposition must have been false ; that Jesus cannot have commanded the institution of a fixed rite modelled on his own last Supper-meal ; that whatever impulse he may have given to the subsequent adoption of a Supper-celebration by his followers, that celebration grew and developed among them, not after the manner of a rite authoritatively fixed in form and content, but rather after the manner of a living organism that develops by adaptation to an ever-changing environment ; and that our five divergent formularies are simply deposits from a few of the diverse forms which the celebration took in different localities. This is the nature of the conclusion reached in this book, but for more positive reasons than as a counsel of despair. Even the central celebration of the Church's worship was not exempt from the Spirit's law of liberty.

To us it may seem strange that Paul and other leaders of the Church should have been willing to commit the control of its worship to a power so incalculable as the Spirit, which was like the wind, blowing where it listeth.

Paul soon discovered some of the dangers it involved ; the church at Corinth was specially turbulent. Yet he does not seem to have wavered in his confidence in the Spirit's leading. We cannot conceive his weighing a suggestion to set up some committee of Apostles or other leaders, to determine authoritatively upon questions of worship. He would have repudiated such a suggestion as a weak reversion to the dead system of Law. He will have no authority except that of the Spirit, or of the living Christ. He rarely makes appeal even to the authority of the *words* of Jesus. True, he is glad to have at hand some clear word from Him when he has some knotty problem of church discipline to resolve.[1] But when dealing with matters of everyday conduct, he dispenses with all such support ; as for instance, in *Romans* xii. and xiii., and *1 Corinthians* xiii., where his exhortations pour from him in a fiery stream, melodious in their phrasing, amazingly sure and confident in their cleaving to the heart of the greatest principles, proclaiming him to be a man whose mind did not work with particular laws, and maxims, and rules of conduct, even though spoken by Jesus, but had gathered these into its own fires and now gave them forth again, glowing and fused into living principles of conduct suited to the needs of the hour. Of the words of Jesus Paul makes little use, because for him the Spirit of Jesus is everything, and he trusts to it wholly.

And he trusts to it in everything. Though the Galatians had shown themselves to be an untutored and fitful people, yet he says to them confidently : " Walk in the Spirit, and ye shall not fulfil the desires of the flesh." [2] Such high-pitched idealism seems glaringly out of keeping with the moral capacity of those to whom it was addressed ; yet Paul did not hesitate. If men possess the Spirit, renewing their minds and giving them a sure sense of what God's will is, then they will want to do it. That was what Paul meant by Freedom. It was the capacity for doing just what we want to do, combined with the gift of wanting

[1] 1 Cor. vii. 25.   [2] Gal. v. 16.

to do only what pleases God. And this latter is a gift from the Spirit that renews men's minds.[1]

These wider considerations are relevant as showing how deeply rooted and how thoroughgoing was the belief in the Spirit. There was no domain of life where its right to control was not recognised, and where the fact of its control was not experienced. And though it must remain to us an astonishing and humbling experience to observe the utter confidence with which the growing Church committed her whole life to the Spirit's guiding, yet, once we have grasped the truth of this, it seems quite natural and indeed inevitable that she should have surrendered the control of her worship to the same Power. Nor is it surprising that she should have continued to reject the restraints of set forms and orders in worship, until, towards the close of the century, the influence of the Spirit began to wane, and many of its functions were gathered into the hands of the advancing powers of ecclesiastical system and authority.

Certain advantages were secured for the worship through its freedom from restraint. Here we specify two :

(1) The worship was kept flexible, and capable of easy adaptation to the needs of widely differing localities and races ; while these, in their turn, contributed to it some touches of their peculiar genius, which thus passed into its accumulating stores. We find ample proof of this in the rich variety, both of form and content, which distinguishes the great Liturgies that emerged later in the wide-flung provinces of the Church.

(2) Within the individual Worship-assemblies, the creative impulses were stimulated in the highest degree. The conduct of worship was not restricted to the few ; it was open to the many. Each member was encouraged and, it would seem, expected to take part. " When you meet together, each contributes something—a song of

[1] Rom. xii. 2.

praise, a lesson, a revelation, a *tongue*, an interpretation." [1]
The community of goods, which appears to have broken
down on the economic side, was firmly established here.
Each threw his contribution into the common store, and,
while enriching it, was himself enriched. For when he
yielded himself to the impulses of the Spirit, faculties of
mind and heart and soul which had hitherto lain dormant
sprang to life. Often we have wondered, when wrestling
with some difficult passage of Paul, how it came about
that the young congregations at Rome, or Corinth, or in
Galatia, composed for the most part of quite ordinary
people, should have been able to understand and to
appreciate letters which are so far from being food for
babes. A large part of the explanation is to be found in
the character of the worship-assemblies to which they
were addressed. These bracing gusts of enthusiasm
which blew upon the bands of worshippers whipped their
capacities into their fullest stride. There, common men
rose to their best—rose even beyond any best they had
hitherto disclosed ; and the contributions they made to
the worship were, we may well believe, of no common order.
The thought of the Church must have been vastly enriched,
and its development greatly accelerated, though the enlist-
ment into its service of so many different minds—minds
which, for the most part, were working at their fullest
stretch under the impulses of the Spirit of God.

[1] I Cor. xiv. 26.

CHAPTER VI

Historical Sketch of Forms and Customs of Worship

A. THE ORIGINAL PALESTINIAN CHURCH

" They devoted themselves to the instruction
given by the apostles and to fellowship, breaking
bread and praying together. Awe fell on every one,
and many wonders and signs were performed by the
apostles in Jerusalem. The believers all kept together ;
they shared all they had with one another, they would
sell their possessions and goods and distribute the
proceeds among all, as any one might be in need.
Day after day they resorted with one accord to the
temple and broke bread together in their homes ;
they ate with a glad and simple heart, praising God
and looked on with favour by all the people. Meanwhile the Lord added the saved daily to their number "
(Acts ii. 42-47).

THIS account of the founding of the Church and
the beginnings of its Worship is generally accepted
as embodying an authentic tradition. It may be that
the writer idealises the situation somewhat—the picture
at the beginning of the sixth chapter is less attractive ; but
there is no good reason to question the substance of his
record. For brevity's sake, it will be sufficient if we
summarise in the next paragraph the general conclusions of one of the most recent writers on this passage,
Foakes-Jackson in his *Commentary on Acts*.[1]

As a consequence of what happened on the day of
Pentecost, the followers of Jesus at Jerusalem formed

[1] *Moffatt's New Testament Commentary*, 1931.

themselves into a compact religious association. It was
the natural thing for a body of Jews like them to do.
All over the Græco-Roman world, Jews had been combining in synagogues ; in Jerusalem itself there were
synagogues under the shadow of the temple. " Possibly,
therefore, the rise of the Christian Church simply as a new
synagogue would cause no surprise ; and if its members,
like the Essenes, had religious customs of their own, this
would be regarded as perfectly natural. Indeed, in *Acts*
the writer insists that the new society was regarded favour-
ably by the people." [1]   It is not easy to define with clearness the attitude of the high authorities in Jerusalem to
the new cause ; but there appears to be little room for
doubt as to the main outcome, which is what concerns
us here. The new society was tolerated ; its members
were left free, with only partial and occasional exceptions,
to live their lives openly, to take part in the temple worship,
and to develop and extend their religious fellowship.

(1) *Continued participation in the Jewish worship.*—" Day
after day they resorted with one accord to the temple."
This would be for a twofold purpose—to receive instruction
from the apostles, and to take part in the temple worship.
For the former of these purposes they gathered in one or
other of these halls, or porches, in which Jesus himself
had taught. There they sat round their leaders to hear
them teach, even as Moslems may still be seen in the
mosques of Cairo or Jerusalem, seated in a group round a
teacher of the Koran, reverently repeating the sacred
words after him. " They devoted themselves to the
instructions given by the Apostles." In addition to this
they took part in the worship of the temple. In the
third chapter of *Acts* we find Peter and John on their way
to the temple for the afternoon hour of prayer. It is not
stated, either in *Acts* or the *Gospels*, that Jesus or his
disciples took part in the sacrificial worship. Whether
they did so is still a debated question. Oesterley,[2] for

[1] P. 21.

[2] *The Jewish Background of the Christian Liturgy*, chap. iii.

instance, thinks that Bartlet is too extreme when he asserts that Jesus took little or no interest in the sacrificial side of the temple worship ; though Oesterley adds that the synagogue worship was more congenial to him. In any event, the main point for our present purpose is clear. After his death, his disciples continued to share in the temple prayers. They had no feeling, as yet, that they ought to break with the old religion, as though it had been superseded by the new. They simply continued their old habits of Jewish worship ; retained the Jewish practice of stated prayers, morning, afternoon, and at sunset ; feeling that these, so far as they went, provided a worthy vehicle for their Christian devotions.

Whether, in addition to frequenting the temple, they also attended one or other of the synagogues in Jerusalem, we do not know. It is possible, nay probable, that they did so. There they would engage in the simple synagogue forms of Scripture-reading and interpretation, followed by Prayer and Praise to God.

To sum up. *On one side their worship remained Jewish.* Their Scripture was the Old Testament ; their prayers were the same prayers they had been taught to pray before ever they had heard of Jesus. These were facts of great importance in shaping the further development.

(2) *Distinctively Christian Worship.*—They " broke bread and prayed together " : " they broke bread together in their own homes ; they ate with a glad and simple heart praising God, and looked on with favour by all the people." Here is something quite new. They are no longer in the temple, mixed in a company of other worshippers, but are gathered in a closed circle of their own, in some private house in the city. Whether the writer means us to understand that they gathered as one company, now in one house, now in another ; or whether it is meant that they gathered in different houses at the same time, as families or as groups of friends and neighbours, we cannot determine. The former would be the natural and desirable thing, but that it was physically possible in view of their

numbers is doubtful. The main point is clear. This distinctively Christian worship was held in some private house or houses, presumably because there was no other available place of meeting.

We must defer, until the chapters on the Lord's Supper, the closer study of these private and intimate gatherings for the breaking of bread. This method of treatment is imposed on us by the difficulties surrounding the early celebration of the rite ; but it calls for a word of caution here. For the immediate result is that in this present chapter a quite disproportionate prominence will be given to the Jewish side of the worship ; and this will present a false picture of the worship as a whole, unless we are careful to remind ourselves that, all through our period, the Supper-celebration was continuous and almost certainly filled a larger place in worship-thought and experience than did the distinctively Jewish elements. Meanwhile, it must suffice to say that the earliest Supper-celebrations took place in the course of the evening meal, and that there was some symbolism expressing the joyous belief that their meal was a continuation of their fellowship with Jesus. It was a meal in which they believed themselves to be closely united to Him. How frequently it was partaken of we cannot determine. The tone of the narrative, with its suggestions of lively religious impulses, points to a more frequent observance than once a week. Perhaps every evening—but we cannot be certain.

This is the second fact of importance in shaping subsequent development. *They gathered in private, as a company of Christian brothers, round a supper-table which, in some emphatic way, was their Master's own Table.*

Of less distinctive significance was another type of Christian gathering in the early Jerusalem church. Before Pentecost we find the Eleven, with the women and with the brothers of Jesus, gathered in the upper-room, where they " resorted with one accord to prayer." [1] On the day of Pentecost,[2] it was when the disciples were all seated

---

[1] Acts i. 12–14.   [2] ii. 1 f.

together in some house that the Spirit came upon them and they spoke with tongues. We read also of the house of Mary, the mother of John Mark, where a "number had met for prayer." [1] There is no mention in these cases of a breaking of bread ; they suggest, rather, informal meetings for prayer. It is well to note and carry with us this fact, that the Christians of that early time gravitated naturally to the holding of meetings for prayer, which were of an informal and intimate kind.

When the Church expanded beyond Jerusalem, and Christian fellowships were founded in the towns of Palestine and such Gentile cities as Antioch and Damascus, we may assume that the practices of the mother-church were followed in the daughter-churches ; the only difference being that the worship in the temple was replaced by worship in the synagogue in association with the local community of Jews.

We now sum up our survey of the worship of the Palestinian church. For close on twenty years, when the Church was expanding under the leadership of Jerusalem, and before Paul had opened out the greater Gentile world beyond the Taurus, *the worship remained consistently semi-Jewish, semi-Christian*. It was Jewish in its association with the temple and the synagogue ; Christian in its Supper-celebrations and informal meetings for prayer in private houses.

B. THE GENTILE CHURCH

Christianity had moved into the Gentile world, notably in the region of Antioch, considerably before Paul's missionary journeys began. Hellenistic influences of far-reaching import are alleged to have entered the Antioch church ; but we do not consider these meantime, since they are not alleged to have materially influenced the *forms* of worship.

In the Pauline churches a new factor emerged. Although

[1] Acts xii. 12.

the traditional practice of joining in the synagogue worship was continued, it rarely lasted for long. Owing to heat of controversy with the Jews over the observance of the Law, there generally followed a complete breach between church and synagogue. What became of the Jewish side of the worship, when it was thus driven from its *locus* in the synagogue ?

Two alternatives offered themselves.   Either some other place of public meeting might be secured ; or a refuge might be found for the Jewish type of worship by combining it with the Supper-celebration held in a private house.

(1) At Ephesus the former alternative seems to have been available. After three months' association with the synagogue, Paul

> " left it, withdrew his disciples, and continued his argument every day from eleven to four in the lecture-room of Tyrannus. This went on for two years, so that all the inhabitants of Asia, Jews as well as Greeks, heard the word of the Lord." [1]

The lecture-room would doubtless be used for worship as well as for more distinctively propaganda work.

(2) At Troas, on the other hand, the second alternative seems to have been adopted.

> " On the first day of the week we met for the breaking of bread ; Paul addressed them, as he was to leave next day, and he prolonged his address till midnight (there were plenty of lamps in the upper room where we met)." (*Then follows the Eutychus incident.*)   " Then he went upstairs, broke bread and ate ; finally after conversing awhile with them till the dawn, he went away." [2]

The writer is not concerned to describe in detail an act of worship, his concern is rather with the incidents that gathered round it ; but his account suggests a meeting

[1] Acts xix. 8-10 (see *Moffatt*).   [2] xx. 7-11.

which opened, after the Jewish fashion, with Scripture, Homily, and Prayer, and which closed with the Supper. The *locus* is a private house, in the upper-room, or *cenaculum*—dining-room, or guest-chamber—which commonly was on the top-flat and was approached directly by an outside stair.[1] It appears, therefore, that Troas was an instance of a town where no covered place of public meeting was available, and where the worship was held in private houses, the *Word-of-God Service* (as the Germans conveniently call the synagogue type of Christian worship, which is represented to-day by the ordinary Protestant Service) being combined with the Supper-celebration. It is probable that Troas was more typical of the general practice than was Ephesus with its available lecture-room. We read of the house of Gaius as one that gave hospitality to the church of Corinth ; also of the house of Prisca and Aquila.[2] It will be noticed that the Troas type of combined Service, if our reconstruction of it is correct, is closely akin to the Service to be described later by Justin Martyr ; showing at how early a period the standard form of Christian Service was already taking shape.[3]

So far, we have found two contrasts emerging continually from our study : (*a*) the contrast between Jewish and Christian : (*b*) the contrast between public and private in the *locus* of the worship. It remains to notice a third contrast (*c*) between *Sunday* and ordinary days. This has been reserved to the last, because it does not appear to have exercised much influence on worship during

[1] Foakes-Jackson, *op. cit.* p. 6.

[2] Rom. xvi. 23 ; 1 Cor. xvi. 19 ; Rom. xvi. 5.

[3] Confusion may arise from the fact that in James ii. 2 a Christian place of worship is called a *synagogue*. This might seem to imply that, when James wrote, Christians were still in the habit of meeting for worship in a synagogue building. But we find *Hermas* applying the term *synagogue* to a distinctively Christian gathering, and this makes it most probable that James used the term in the same sense. It was quite natural for Jewish Christians to regard their Christian worship-gathering as a *synagogue*. Cf. Streeter, *op. cit.* p. 72 f.

the vigorous and creative period in the first century. Its potent influences came later.

There are few references in the New Testament to Sunday in connection with worship.

(1) 1 Cor. xvi. 2.—Paul suggests that " on the first day of the week " each should lay aside a sum from his weekly gains to help the saints at Jerusalem.

(2) Rev. i. 10.—The seer was " in the Spirit on the Lord's day." This is the first use of the designation " Lord's day," which, as the *Ignatian Letters* show, was established, by the beginning of the second century, as a common designation for the day following the Sabbath.

(3) Acts xx. 7.—It was on " the first day of the week " that the meeting took place at Troas for the breaking of bread. But this may be a mere note of time, and may have no Worship-significance. It may have been that, since Paul dared not start a journey on the Sabbath, he had to delay till sunrise on the following day, and so, it was during the earlier hours of the first day of the week that he held the farewell meeting with his friends.

In (1) and (2) at least we have traces, though vague and indeterminate, of Sunday being already singled out as a special day in connection with Worship.

The reasons for this development are obscure. Deissmann [1] inclines to find in it evidence of conscious protest against the Roman cult of the Emperor with its " Augustus day." Bousset [2] thinks it was the result of growing antagonism towards the Jews, and of a desire to break with their Sabbath. (The later change from the Jewish Fast-days on Monday and Thursday to the Christian Fast-days on Wednesday and Friday would fall into line

[1] *Light from the Ancient East* (1927), p. 359.
[2] *Kyrios Christos* (1913), p. 31.

with this.)   Duchesne [1] attributes the new departure, not
to feelings of antagonism, but to a natural desire to have,
side by side with the Sabbath which they celebrated along
with their Jewish brethren, a day set apart for exclusively
Christian assemblies.   There certainly was no idea of
equating the Sunday with the Sabbath.

> " The idea of imparting to the Sunday the solemnity
> of the Sabbath, with all its exigencies and in particular
> its prohibition of work, was an entirely foreign one to
> the early Christians." [2]

We find in the literature of the second century that by
that time the celebration of Sunday was closely associated
with the belief in the Resurrection on the third day.   The
whole question is still obscure through lack of evidence.

What concerns us specially is to determine whether this
celebration of Sunday had any decisive influence on the
course of the *earlier* worship.   In the *Didachê*,[3] Christians
are enjoined to gather themselves together and break
bread " on the Lord's own day."   Pliny, reporting on the
Christians in his Province, speaks of their habit of holding
worship on a stated day—*stato die*.   These two witnesses
prove that by the beginning of the second century the
Sunday was definitely asserting its place as the most
important day of worship in the week.   In the succeeding
literature we find repeated appeals that Christians should
gather for worship as often as possible.   Origen bids them
gather " to the wells of Scripture " every day if possible,
and not merely on Feast-days and Sundays.[4]   This
suggests, not simply that Sunday was overshadowing the
other days, but that the absence of worship on these days
was deplored as a decline from a better practice.   The

---

[1] *Origins of Christian Worship*, cap. ii.

[2] *Ibid.*   Cf. Rom. xiv. 5 ; Col. ii. 16.

[3] Chapter xiv.

[4] Cyprian recommended daily Communion ;   Hippolytus wrote a
treatise, now lost : *de eucharistia an accipienda quotidie.*

5

evidence indicates that, during the early creative period, there was little or no tendency to exalt the Sunday worship at the expense of everyday worship. The New Testament depicts a remarkably rich and vigorous church life, with the Worship as its animating centre ; and the final impression is of frequent gatherings for worship. It was out of this rich and vigorous worship-life that the special celebration of Sunday emerged, and it would only be by degrees, as the Enthusiasm cooled, that the Sunday would succeed in draining away the worship activities from the other days of the week, and concentrating them upon itself.

C. THE CLASSIC FORM OF CHRISTIAN WORSHIP

Christian Worship attained its standard form before the middle of the second century, as we learn from the description by Justin Martyr of the Sunday Service to which he was accustomed, presumably at Rome, about the year A.D. 150.[1] From his description it will be seen that his Sunday Service was simply the Word-of-God Service followed by the Lord's Supper. The Supper had ceased being a meal ; it was not even conjoined with the partaking of a meal ; it had become a simple ritual act. Otherwise, all the things said and done at Justin's Service had been said and done, in kindred fashion though not always at the one time, since the beginning. Let it be noted also that this second-century Service represents the standard type of Service that was to prevail throughout succeeding ages. The worship of the Church was to experience some strange developments ; but these developments all took place *within* this simple framework. It has never been superseded.

Justin's description is as follows (the translation is Duchesne's) :

"On the day of the Sun, all who live in towns or in the country gather together to one place, and the

[1] *Apology*, i. 67.

memoirs of the Apostles and the writings of the Prophets are read as long as time permits. Then when the reader has ceased, the President speaks, admonishing and exhorting to the imitation of these excellent things. Then all rise together and prayers are offered. At length, as we have already described, prayer being ended, bread and wine and water are brought, and the President offers prayers and thanksgivings to the best of his ability, and the people assent by saying 'Amen': and the distribution is made to each one of his share of the elements which have been blessed, and to those who are not present it is sent by the ministry of the deacons."

The only addition made by Justin to this picture is when he mentions [1] the *kiss of peace*, which was exchanged after the prayers and before the Eucharist. He does not tell us at what time of the day the Service was held ; but it is practically certain that it was in the early morning. Pliny's letter describes the Christians as meeting early in the morning and binding themselves with a *sacrament*. Tertullian (*c.* A.D. 200) says expressly that though the Sacrament of the Eucharist was commanded by our Lord at meal-times, " we take it in assemblies before daybreak." [2] The choice of the early morning hour would be dictated largely by the fact that most worshippers were busy people and had their day's work to do as usual.

Justin's Service is simply the old Word-of-God Service followed by the Lord's Supper, the latter being now dissociated from a meal and celebrated as a simple ritual act. The reason for giving prominence to Justin's account is because it is the earliest deliberate and detailed description of a full Christian Service. Services such as this must have been held long before Justin's day ; probably they became the rule in a church when it separated its Lord's Supper from the evening meal, and in the early years of the century this process of separation had begun. When

---

[1] *Apology*, i. 65.　　　　[2] *De Corona Militis*, chap. iii.

we have studied the Lord's Supper more closely we shall be better able to grasp the situation as a whole. Meantime it should be said that when we survey the whole field of the Worship, from its *terminus a quo* in the Primitive practice of synagogue worship conjoined with a celebration of the Supper to its *terminus ad quem* in the standard model of worship already achieved by Justin's time, and when we observe that the latter is, in form, simply a juxtaposition of the two elements of the former, we get an impression of the sureness of the Guidance which led the Church's worship, during a century of crisis and most varied experience, forward to what was nothing else but a single compacted form of the two simple elements of worship with which she had started on her career at the first.

D. WANING OF THE ENTHUSIASM : STANDARDISING OF THE WORSHIP

It was inevitable that the first Enthusiasm should wane. Psychologically it was inevitable ; because human nature could not for long sustain the tension of those high altitudes of emotion and experience. Historically also it was inevitable ; because certain of the conditions which fostered the Enthusiasm were time-conditions which passed with the passing of the years. One of these conditions, for instance, was the fact that memories of the voice of Jesus of Nazareth still lingered in the ears of living men, and there was abroad still in the Church an overwhelming sense of the *newness* of the Christian experience. It was spring-time, when light was pouring in after darkness and all things were being made new. But spring-time must pass. " In that first age the gospel was literally the good news, but the surprise and exultation of good news can only be felt once."[1] The waning of the Enthusiasm was, therefore, no mere decline from a higher state of things, but a necessary stage in the advance of the cause. The creative period had passed because its work was

[1] E. F. Scott, *The New Testament To-day*, p. 21.

accomplished. Invariably it is the beginning of a religious movement that marks its greatest achievement. " Philosophy, art, literature ascend gradually to their golden age by a long process of thought and experiment. But religion must leap to its goal by an intuition, or it will never reach it." [1] Christianity had already leaped to her goal, and both in her literature and her worship she had struck out her classic forms of expression, which no succeeding age was to transcend. It remained now that she should move down to lower levels, where her task was to consolidate her victories, organise her rich gains, and equip herself for her mission to the world.

The waning of the Enthusiasm was no uniform process, nor one that can be definitely dated or documented. But there is one thing we can say. By about the year A.D. 65 the three great apostolic leaders, Peter, Paul, and James, were dead ; and from that time till the end of the century is one of the darkest periods of Christian history, " illuminated by no great name, and by scarcely any recorded incident." [2] To pass from the year 65 to the year 100 has been compared to passing through a tunnel ; but, we might add, it is the kind of tunnel that pierces a frontier range of mountains ; when we emerge from it we find ourselves in another climate ; the air is cooler and the landscape more ordinary. This is a fair simile for the change from reading Paul's *Epistles* to reading the *Pastoral Epistles*, or Clement's *Epistle*. We have passed from the region of creative Enthusiasm into a region of growing ecclesiastical system and order.

In the Johannine writings we are not sensible of this acute change ; and in the *Apocalypse* and the *Ignatian Letters* the authentic notes of Enthusiasm still ring out. But in the rest of the New Testament and in the great bulk of the succeeding literature the change is manifest.

[1] *The New Testament To-day*, p. 22.
[2] E. F. Scott, *The Epistle to the Hebrews*. p. 195 f.

A detailed account of the change and of the evidence for it will be found in E. F. Scott's *The Spirit in the New Testament*, chap. vi. Summarised, the evidence points to the conception of the Spirit having been relegated to a subordinate place. Rarely, if ever, is it a central interest of the Christian life. It is still referred to in passing, as the source of the " spiritual gifts " : [1] as the vehicle of revelation, especially of that given in the Old Testament.[2] It is more closely associated with stated ordinances, baptism, and the laying on of hands : [3] it safeguards the belief given in the Church Confession.[4] Referring in particular to the *Pastoral Epistles*, the writer says :

> " The Spirit does not now come direct from God, but is vested in the Church, and is transmitted through its duly appointed officers. . . . Before the century was over the Church had formed itself into an institution. . . . It preserved the earlier doctrine of the Spirit, but subordinated it to the conception of the Church . . . " (p. 228 f.).

Accompanying the decline of the enthusiasm, there were *positive factors* which co-operated in the " cooling and hardening process," as it has been described. The increasing size of congregations, as they grew from being compact house-assemblies into looser aggregations of people less intimately bound to each other ; the growing need for organisation and order, and the resulting emergence to power of the men of affairs in place of the men of the Spirit—these hastened the process. Prophets who once had stood second only to Apostles in the esteem of the Church were now relegated to a lower place ; indeed, by the time of the *Didachê*, although the true prophet was still honoured and entrusted with the presidency at the

---

[1] Heb. ii. 4 ; 1 Pet. i. 12.
[2] Heb. iii. 7, ix. 8, x. 15 ; 1 Pet. i. 11.
[3] 1 Tim. iv. 14 ; 2 Tim. i. 6.
[4] 2 Tim. i. 14.

eucharistic celebration and with liberty to pray there " as he will," yet Prophets, as a class, were under a cloud ; for there were many false prophets about, and watchful discrimination was called for.[1] The Bishop, on the other hand, steadily advanced in prestige and power, and became the leading figure in worship. Bousset maintains that it was the control of worship that was the first rung of the ladder on which he mounted to his pre-eminence in the Church.[2] Streeter holds that an examination of the evolution of Church Order at this period suffices, if not to prove, at least to make probable the fact of a " slow and steady movement."

> " It is a movement away from the state of things implied in *1 Corinthians*—where pre-eminence in the Church depends on the *personal* possession of some spiritual gift (of which ' government ' is one of the least esteemed)—and towards a state of things where importance is attached to the holding of an *office* invested with recognised authority." [3]

Within the Worship, this waning of the Enthusiasm was attended by a process of standardising and systematising. We can indicate certain new tendencies which now begin to appear.

(1) *The layman is superseded by the official* ; the layman surrendering his functions in the conduct of worship through lack of spiritual initiative, while the official gathers these surrendered functions into his own hands. Ignatius writes of " the prayer of the Bishop and the whole church," [4] showing how prominent a position the Bishop had already gained in the worship. The eucharistic prayer appears to have been the first element to be strictly reserved to the President ; while the prayers preceding the Eucharist continued for longer to be free prayers by individual members.[5] Although, in the end, all prayers

[1] Chapter xi. [2] *Kyrios Christos* (1913), p. 340.
[3] *Op. cit.* 83. [4] *Eph.* v. 2.
[5] Perhaps Justin's Service contains both types.

passed into the hands of the officiating Bishops and Deacons,
yet for long an exception was made in favour of laymen of
high spiritual endowment, who were allowed to contribute
prayers of their own.[1]

(2) *Worship, but especially the prayers, tended to become
stereotyped.* In the early worship, prayers had been com-
pletely free. The Enthusiasm brooked no restraints, and
all true prayers were Spirit-inspired. Although in practice
the man praying might draw upon the rich and familiar
liturgical stores of the Old Testament and the synagogue
ritual,[2] that was a matter for himself ; he remained free
to pray " as he would." It is from this early practice that
evangelical revivals throughout the history of Christendom
have derived their charter of freedom in prayer. Tertullian, who championed the charismatic Montanist
movement, claims for Christians that they pray freely and
without restraint : " sine monitore, quia de pectore
oramus " : " ut quisque de proprio ingenio posset." [3]

The subduing of this original freedom was a long process.
Even when the conduct of public worship had become the
exclusive business of the Bishop or other official, the composition and the length of the prayer were left to his own
discretion. In Justin's Sunday Service the President
prays " to the best of his ability." But the fact that the
prayers had now passed into the hands of one or two
officials tended inevitably to the stereotyping and standardising of prayer. Although a Bishop might speak his
prayer " free," he could not be in a position to produce
something new every time ; he would tend to fall into
habitual thought-sequences, and to repeat familiar turns
of expression and phrase ; in this way he would gradually
be led to build up a ritual of his own. A good example
may be seen in Clement's prayer.[4] The Liturgies of

[1] Heiler, *Das Gebet*, p. 435.

[2] The synagogue ritual was in large measure stereotyped and
familiar, though never at this time permitted to be written down.
Ibid. p. 437.

[3] *Apology*, 30 : 39.   [4] See *infra*, Chapter VIII.

the later Church are deeply indebted to the prayers of
the synagogue ; and some part of that debt was incurred,
no doubt, at this period when the individual Bishops
had to maintain the worship of their churches out of
their own prayer resources ; very naturally they would
fall back upon the rich stores of the Jewish worship. An
auxiliary factor hastening the process of standardisation
was the practice for prominent leaders of worship to write
out and disseminate [1] " pattern-prayers." These pattern-
prayers were to be used, not as binding formularies, but
as models for the inexperienced or for the unready of
speech. Perhaps the *Didachê* prayers for use at the
Eucharist are examples of such model-prayers. Heiler
summarises the after-development thus :

> " Till well on into the third century free prayer
> prevailed. By the fifth century we find everywhere
> fixed ordinances of public worship and compulsory
> prayer-formularies. The leader of prayer no longer
> prays *de pectore*, but recites a sacred text from memory,
> or reads it out of a ritual book. ' [2]

(3) But before this result was attained, there was
necessary a further process which made for *uniformity,
not merely in the practice of the single church, but also in the
practice of groups of churches over a region or province.*
When a church was first founded, we may take it that the
main lines of its worship were laid down for it by the
example of its missionary-founder. But within those
limits there must have been much freedom of development,
resulting in diversity as between church and church.
With the growth and expansion of the Church, however,
organisation became inevitable Some leading church in
a region seems to have been accorded a hegemony, and
naturally so if on her rested the glory of having been
founded by an Apostle or closely associated with one.

[1] For an interesting pointer to the methods of Christian publication and circulation, see Hermas, *Visions* ii. 4, 3.

[2] *Op. cit.* 437.

From her the surrounding churches received guidance and example as to what was proper to a Christian church.   The letter written by Clement from the church of Rome to the church of Corinth is a case of a church with great traditions taking upon herself the privilege of advising another church with traditions almost as great. And so the process towards uniformity moved forward ; hastened, we may be sure, by the frequent visits of individuals to churches in other districts, or other provinces, or other continents where they were travelling. These guests of a church would feel at home, and make it be seen that they felt at home, largely in the degree in which they found the worship of their hosts to be in keeping with the familiar and much-loved worship of their own church at home. In such ways there grew up within the Church a public opinion making for uniformity, which accelerated the standardisation of worship, towards which so many factors were co-operating.

PART II

THE WORSHIP IN DETAIL

WORD AND SACRAMENTS

CHAPTER VII

THE WORD-OF-GOD SERVICE

W E have now had a general survey of the more prominent features of the early Worship. It stood forth before its world as a closely-compacted Fellowship at once Social and Religious : while, within itself, it was vitalised and controlled at every point by the Spirit of God. We have seen how vivid and realistic were the believers' experiences of God's presence through His Spirit, and we are in a position to realise something of the unconstrained freedom of their worship with its tense notes at once of confident joy and adoring awe. Their worship came from them as its song comes from the bird ; it was a spontaneous outflow from within. Everywhere we are made sensible of an incomparable freshness, and vigour, and creative power.

We must now address ourselves to more detailed aspects of the Worship, but we shall find that this closer study amply confirms the general impressions we have already gained.

Our historical sketch of the Worship's development in form and practice showed how consistently it continued to move about its two original *foci*—the old, Jewish Word-of-God Service, and the new, Christian Lord's Supper. We have seen also that the final and standard form of Divine Service was firmly consolidated at Rome as early as the

time of Justin the Martyr about the middle of the second
century, and that it was simply a welding-together of the
two original elements which had been the Church's possession from the first.   Our task, therefore, in the next eight
chapters will be to review in detail the component parts
of this standard Sunday Service.   The present and the
two succeeding chapters will be occupied with the Word-of-
God Service, that is to say, with the *Reading and
Interpretation of Scripture, Preaching, Prayer*, and *Praise*.
The subsequent chapters will be devoted to the *Lord's
Supper*.   A concluding chapter in this series will deal
with *Baptism*, this being reserved to the last because,
through its being a rite primarily for the individual rather
than for the worshipping community as a whole, Baptism
lay somewhat aside from the main stream of the Worship.

In this study of the detail, we will continue to follow
our two main guiding principles.   First, we will con-
centrate on the early creative period which did not long
survive the passing of the great Apostles, Paul, Peter, and
James ;   contenting ourselves with an indication of the
broad lines of the subsequent development.   Further, we
will endeavour to keep the worshipper himself at the
centre of our picture.   We have found reason to think
that his worship-practices were not things imposed upon
him by authority from without, but were spontaneous
growths from within, from his experience of God in Christ
and in His Spirit.   Naturally, he made use of old forms
of worship inherited from his pre-Christian past to express
his new experience, but the influence of these forms in
colouring his experience was small, compared with the
influence of his experience in revitalising the forms.
Accordingly we will not be content with knowing *how* he
spoke and acted when at worship ; we will try, even more
insistently, to understand *why* he spoke and acted thus.
What was he thinking, and feeling, and experiencing that
he should have elected to express himself in just this
fashion rather than in some other ?

As the Christian Word-of-God Service was, in its form and order, a direct copy of the Jewish worship of the synagogue, some brief account of the *origins of the synagogue* will be helpful at this point.

Too little is known of these origins to justify precise statements. We know that the synagogue was a product of exilic Judaism. Elbogen suggests that it was the reading of Scripture that supplied the first impulse for these synagogue assemblies, which were the first of their kind in the history of man's worship. Exiled to a land which was unclean and given over to demons, and debarred from approaching God in the ancestral manner of their temple worship, the Jews gathered to read their Scriptures, which brought home to them their responsibility for their disasters, but also showed to them, through the door of repentance, new vistas of hope. But whether or not the Scriptures provided the first rallying-point for their worship, it is generally agreed that it was *Prayer* that came to be its most significant and expressive element.

> " Jeremiah was the spiritual founder of the synagogue. . . . The conviction which gave vitality to the synagogue—that the Jew could live a loyal Jew without sacrifice, but could not so live without prayer—derived directly from the prophet." [1]
>
> " The prayer-songs written by others in dependence on Jeremiah, giving expression to the exile-experiences whether of suffering or confidence, rang out in these synagogue gatherings. The Psalter became the prayer book of the exilic church. The force and passion of Jeremiah's praying spirit passed through the Psalms into the piety of the exilic church." [2]

A final quotation from Elbogen will indicate the historical significance of the synagogue worship.

> " The synagogue introduced a new kind of worship.

[1] A. C. Welch, *Jeremiah*, p. 248.
[2] Heiler, *Das Gebet*, p. 42.

. . . It was the first time in the history of mankind
that regular gatherings for worship were held in places
which had no other consecration than that which
the gatherings of believers gave them. It was a
worship which freed itself from all hitherto customary
usages among the peoples, and renounced all material
adjuncts, like sacrifices and formal offerings, and
discarded representation through priests, and placed
at the centre of worship man with his inner spiritual
life." [1]

That the young Christian Church should have taken
over and retained the simple synagogue service need
occasion no surprise. What better foundation could be
found for an act of Worship than the Word of God?
Or what other Form could have provided a larger liberty
for inspired speech and prayer? Indeed the Form is so
simple and so natural, so congenial to a sincere worship
and so hospitable to free impulses of the Spirit that we
cannot help feeling that Christianity would have discovered it for herself if the old, exile-chastened Jews had
not anticipated her; and it would not greatly surprise
us if new evidence came to light showing that it was the
normal rule for Christian worship of all kinds, eucharistic,
propagandist, or other, to commence in this manner.
One main reason for the scarcity of direct reference to
Worship in the New Testament lay in its being so simple
and pliable in form, and altogether so much the natural
and congenial thing that it called for no special comment
from those who were steeped in it. No one thinks or
talks much about the air he breathes, so long as it is fresh
and pure.

READING AND INTERPRETATION OF SCRIPTURE

There are many threads of evidence showing that the
Church simply took over the synagogue custom of reading

[1] Quoted by Heiler, *op. cit.* p. 474.

portions from the Old Testament books of the Law and of the Prophets;[1] but the earliest detailed account comes from the passage already quoted from Justin.[2]

From this it appears:

(a) The passages were not yet fixed in length; the choice of them may have been left to the reader and the length determined by him. In the synagogue, any one, even a boy of twelve, might be called on to read,[3] and possibly this tradition maintained itself during New Testament times.

(b) By Justin's time the New Testament writings were finding a place in worship alongside the Old Testament Scriptures. The earliest mention of the reading of a Christian writing at worship is in *Colossians* : [4] " and when this letter has been read to you, see that it is also read in the church of the Laodiceans." So far as we know such a Christian writing was not regarded as holy Scripture during the New Testament period. The Old Testament *Law* and *Prophets* still retained that unique position.

(c) It would seem that the reader and the " preacher " —if we may call him so—were not as a rule the same person. In that event the reader would sometimes simply read; at other times he might add something of his own by way of interpretation, but when he did so he would probably confine himself, on the analogy of the synagogue practice, to a kind of paraphrase or running commentary on the text. The *admonishing and exhorting*, on the other hand, was something different ; more of the nature of a homily, or sermon, based on the passage read. Sometimes, no doubt, the preacher would himself act as reader. However, we have no direct information on the early Christian practice, and perhaps the most that we can say with confidence is that the reading of Scripture was normally accompanied by a commentary, or by a freer and more extended homily based on it, or by both.

[1] See Oesterley, *Jewish Background*, chaps. ii.–v.
[2] See p. 66 f.   [3] Oesterley, *op. cit.* p 117.
[4] iv. 16.

Three matters of more general interest call for notice.

(1) *The Early Christian attitude to the Old Testament.*
The Old Testament was the acknowledged Scripture of
the Church, even as it was of the synagogue. There was
no time when it was not regarded as the Word of God,
speaking with the same authority with which it had
spoken in the old Religion. More than that : as early as
Paul we find the conviction freely expressed that the Old
Testament was a specifically Christian book.[1] Its warnings
and encouragements, he says, " were all written down of
old for our instruction." Christianity annexed the Old
Testament as its own in the fullest sense. This becomes
abundantly clear in Clement's *Letter.*

> " Clement's use of Scripture rests upon the pre-
> supposition, general among Christians, that the Old
> Testament was the one unique book, given by God
> to the Christians, yes, specifically to the Christians.
> Its words could claim absolute authority. . . . It
> would be a quite inadequate statement of the case to
> say that the Old Testament, in whole or in part, was
> *still* valid for Christians ; as though such recognition
> of it had been the result of reflection, or as though
> the possession of that wonderful and infallible book
> had not seemed in the eyes of the Church to be one
> of the most obvious and attractive of the advantages
> of the new religion. We cannot too forcibly impress
> upon our minds the fact that there was not at first
> the least idea that a time would arrive when a second
> holy Scripture would come into being and take its
> place alongside of, nay, superior to the first." [2]

Harnack [3] writes in glowing terms of the commanding
prestige of the Book not only within the Church, but also
among cultivated outsiders, for many of whom it became
the bridge that carried them over to Christianity.

---

[1] Rom. xv. 4 ; 1 Cor. x. 11, ix. 10; 2 Cor. i. 20.

[2] Wrede, *Untersuchungen zum ersten Clemensbrief,* 75 f.

[3] *Mission und Ausbreitung* (1902), 205 f.

" The possession of their sacred scriptures, descended from an antiquity by the side of which the beginnings of Greek philosophy were modern, and derived from divine revelation, made a doubly profound impression upon an age which turned its eyes to the ancients for wisdom and to heaven for a truth beyond the attainment of Reason." [1]

(2) *In New Testament times, knowledge of Scripture must have been derived principally from its use in Worship.* The ground for this inference is the strong probability that the Book had no wide currency as a private possession in the hands of Christians generally. The evidence has been collected by Harnack, and, briefly summarised, is to this effect.[2]

(*a*) There was no theoretical restraint upon the reading and study of Scripture. In Judaism the Book was to be found in the school, the family, and the study ; we have the New Testament instance of the eunuch with his copy of *Isaiah*. When Jews became Christians they would continue their private use of Scripture, probably with even more zeal than before since now they sought proofs of the Messiahship of Jesus. For Gentile Christians the Septuagint translation into Greek was available.

(*b*) On the other hand, although custom, common sense, and principle alike pointed to a free private use of Scripture, yet such use was not common among Christians. There is no clear mention of it anywhere in the New Testament. When Timothy is admonished : "Attend to your Scripture-reading, your preaching, and your teaching, till I come," [3] the reference seems to be to the public reading of Scripture. When *Acts* says of the Bereans that " they were perfectly ready to receive the Word and made a daily study of the Scriptures to see if it was really as Paul said," [4] it appears to point to a study

---

[1] G. F. Moore, *History of Religion*, ii. 521 f.
[2] *Bible Reading in the Early Church.*
[3] 1 Tim. iv. 13.   [4] Acts xvii. 11.

6

of the synagogue copies, which were accessible to the individual. The silence of the New Testament is probably no accident but reflects the actual conditions. There was no large store of copies available owing to the undeveloped state of the publishing trade and to the fact that copies had to be made by hand ; and though the copies on the market were not highly expensive, they would be beyond the reach of most Christians.

The conclusion is that although the genius of Christianity was wholly in favour of a complete publicity of the Word, yet the private possession of copies cannot have been widespread ; and believers must have depended for their knowledge of Scripture mainly upon the teaching of their church. Probably this teaching was communicated for the most part through the reading and interpretation of Scripture during worship. *A priori*, it is improbable that in the early days there was *systematic* instruction, in classes apart from the worship-assemblies. The first evidence of such appears towards the end of the century in connection with Baptism ;[1] but in the earlier period the conditions of Enthusiasm, combined with the lack of time and leisure, would militate against a matured system of instruction. This whole matter, however, presents a highly complex and difficult problem which is of special importance in its bearing on the early dissemination of knowledge of the life and teaching of Jesus and on the origins of our Synoptic Gospels. This problem cannot be entered on here. We must be content with the conclusion that in the earlier days knowledge of the Scriptures was disseminated chiefly through public instruction given by the Church ; we cannot as yet hope for agreed conclusions as to the precise manner in which it was given.

(3) *The spirit and method which controlled the interpretation of Scripture* is entirely out of accord with our modern ideas of scientific accuracy. It is not merely that Paul, for instance, is content to argue from the

---

[1] Heb. vi. 2 : *Didachê*, i.–vi.

Greek translation of the Old Testament without evincing any desire to check it by the original Hebrew ; he does not even show a desire to master the context of his passages, or to discover their original meaning for the man who wrote them. His whole concern is with some hidden meaning that is believed to lie underneath the words and to be their truest meaning, discernible, however, only by a mind illuminated through the Spirit of Christ. Thus, he draws a sharp contrast between the reading of the scriptures in the synagogue and the reading of the same scriptures in the Christian worship.[1] In the synagogue a veil lies on the hearts of the hearers, and though they hear the words they cannot understand their real import ; but in the Christian assembly the veil is withdrawn and the light of God's truth can reach the mind and transform the life. There are several examples in the New Testament of this discovery of hidden meanings lying behind the natural, and indeed authentic meaning of a text.[2] The example from *1 Corinthians* is familiar, and shows clearly how misleading this allegorical method could be.

" It is written in the law of Moses, *You must not muzzle an ox when he is treading the grain.* Is God thinking here about cattle ? Or is he speaking purely for our sakes ? Assuredly for our sakes. This word was written for us. . . ."

Paul will have it that when God forbids the muzzling of the ox as it treads out the grain, He must have been thinking of the needs of labourers in His coming Kingdom ; for it is out of the question that He could be thinking about cattle. Actually, there is in this Old Testament prohibition of the muzzling of the ox a fine thought of the wide mercy of God ; and even a city-bred man like Paul could scarcely have failed to do it justice, had not his mind been led astray by his presupposition that beneath the surface-meaning of Scripture God had deposited

[1] 2 Cor. iii. 14.
[2] Rom. x. 8 ; Gal. iii. 16, iv. 24 ; 1 Cor. ix. 9 f.

hidden truths which only a Christ-enlightened mind could discover.

In all this, Paul and other Christian interpreters—notably the author of *Hebrews*—were merely following a thought-fashion of their day, which prevailed alike among bible-readers in the Jewish synagogue and philosophers of the Greek Stoa. The *midrash*, or popular teaching of the synagogue, which has been described as " the poetry of the Talmud," and which is defined in the *Jewish Encyclopædia* as

> " an exegesis which, going more deeply than the literal sense, attempts to penetrate into the spirit of the scriptures, to examine the text from all sides, and thereby to derive interpretations which are not immediately obvious,"

was free to use fancy as much as it pleased, so long as it was " unto edification." The allegorising employed by the Stoic philosophers followed similar lines, but seems to have been of older standing than that of the synagogue, and was even more thoroughgoing. The *raison d'être* of such a method is not far to seek. Alike in Greek Mythology and in the Old Testament there was much ancient matter of which the meaning was either lost or had become offensive to the moral instinct of a more advanced age. Scarcely was it possible to salve that archaic material except by allegorising it. Probably that was the only way by which, in that age, respect for sacred traditions could have been preserved and the continuity of religious thought maintained.

Accordingly, when we have said the worst that our modern thought can urge against this method of interpretation, we come back to this, that only through such casuistry of faith could the Old Testament have continued to hold its commanding position as the sacred and infallible Word of God. Although Paul was unfortunate enough to meddle with the muzzled ox, and so to exhibit his allegorical method at its worst, yet we must acknowledge that the method did far more good than harm. It preserved the Old Testament as God's Word, and secured for the Church the freedom of a rich world of spiritual thought and experience, where a Spirit-quickened mind could find the bread and water of life in abundance, without needing to resort to allegory. And if some regions of that ancient Jewish thought-world had become barren or positively noxious for the spirit of man, it would scarcely be wise to cavil overmuch at a method of interpretation which enabled the quickened imagination of the Church to invest these regions with fertilities and salubrities which they did not in themselves possess. A more scientific treatment of the Old Testament might easily have turned the book into a derision for that age ; or it might, in another way, have forged out of it a fetter and hindrance to progress. As it was, the ancient Scriptures continued to be the Word of God ; and when they were read in worship, they were felt to be speaking home to the soul with the voice of the life-giving Spirit of Christ Himself.

PREACHING

Our quotation from Justin showed that it was the custom in his church that when the reader had finished the President spoke, " admonishing, and exhorting to the imitation of these excellent things." We shall call this " preaching," although it was probably a less elaborate and formal exercise than the word suggests to us. It is well, however, to hold to the generic term, since there is no doubt that, just as this homily, or address, had grown out of the simple commentary on the read Scripture, so it became in its turn the progenitor of the more developed preaching of later days.

We possess no verbal report of any example of New Testament preaching. The reports of the apostolic preaching in *Acts*—as at Jerusalem, Cæsarea, Pisidian Antioch, Lystra, Athens—are at the best mere summaries of what was said, and contain little of the vivid detail or of the outflashing of the preacher's personality which must have been large part of the secret of their effectiveness. Besides, these are reports for the most part of the *missionary preaching* to outsiders, which is to be distinguished from the preaching within the Christian worship. Probably the missionary preaching approached closer to our ideas of preaching. When the preacher faced an audience that were strangers to him and to Christ, he had before him a definite task, restricted within fairly well-defined limits. First, he had to bring his hearers to repentance, and as a rule he did this by rousing in them a sense of urgency and crisis in presence of an impending doom ; then he would present to them the great Redeemer with whom refuge was to be found. Now, before this double message could get home, a variety of prejudices, or superstitions, or indifferences, as the case might be, had to be overcome ; consequently, the work must have been attended by a constant effort of thought to discover the best means of overcoming these, and of presenting the message in a form that would not repel. There would, therefore, be built up, in the course of experience, structures of approved argument and appeal which probably were not greatly dissimilar in form from the thought-out preaching of later days.

But it is unlikely that this was the character of the preaching at the Worship of believers. Later, when the Enthusiasm had cooled, and when larger congregations gathered in more commodious buildings, the conditions became favourable for the growth of the more deliberate and premeditated sermon. But in the early worship, held frequently in private houses, the speaking must have been less formal, more intimate and spontaneous. In the missionary gatherings, the speaking was the decisive factor, for it was through it that the Word of God was brought home to men with power. But in Worship proper, the Preaching does not seem to have had this all-prominent place. It was Prayer and the Lord's Supper that were felt to be the culminating points of worship, preaching being ancillary and preparatory to these. Consequently, even if it was an early custom for the President to deliver a set homily or address after the reading of Scripture (and of this there is no clear evidence), it is unlikely that it bore the features of a premeditated and strenuous effort ; at the most it would be regarded as *primus inter pares* alongside of the other utterances, by this man or that, elicited by the Spirit during the course of the worship. No doubt it was different when Paul, or some other special personage, was present ; at Troas Paul preached so long that Eutychus fell asleep. But we may feel certain that neither the sleeping nor the extended preaching were customary things in the worship of the early Church.

At this point we remind ourselves how seriously the control of the Spirit was taken in the early worship. Scholars of our generation are continually admonishing us —in the words of one of the greatest of them :

> " We cannot be too earnest in familiarising ourselves with the thought that early Christianity did not conceive the new life as being merely a new way of thinking and living for a man, but rather as being a wonderful endowment of him with new powers direct from God." [1]

The drama of salvation was not wrought out merely within the mind and will ; it was conceived more objectively than that—as the descent upon the man of powers coming from above. " God's realm does not show itself in talk, but in power." [2] The preacher of that day was not tempted, as the modern preacher often is, to regard the burden of convincing others as resting finally upon the quality of his thought and speech ; it rested elsewhere, with the Spirit of God. When Paul says that he came to Corinth, resolved to be " ignorant of everything except Jesus Christ, and Jesus Christ the crucified," there can be

[1] J. Weiss, *Urchristentum*, p. 188.
[2] As Moffatt translates 1 Cor. iv. 20.

little doubt as to what he meant. He had determined to shun the methods of the rhetorician and the philosopher, and to entrust to the Spirit of God the demonstration of the truth of his message. So he would prepare for preaching, largely by steeping himself in the consciousness of his own salvation and of his own debt to Christ ; and when he faced his hearers, he would simply give out to them what lay closest to his heart, speaking of the Christ he knew who had loved him and given himself for him, and then standing aside to let the message do its own work as God brought it home to the lives He had chosen for His own.

It is possible that in such a passage as the following we have echoes of the warm directness and intimacy with which Paul spoke among his own Christian people :

> " We have peace with God through our Lord Jesus Christ. Through him we have access into this grace wherein we stand, and rejoice in the hope of the glory of God. . . . And our hope never puts us to shame, because the love of God floods our hearts through the Holy Spirit which has been given to us." [1]

When people listened to speech like this, their first and their last impression must have been that here was a man who indeed had found peace with God. Even though we possessed a verbatim report of this earliest preaching, still we would not comprehend its full power ; because its essential power lay, not in its matter nor in its method, but in something else which the written word can never capture—the dynamic of personalities that had surrendered themselves joyfully to God. Thus, at least, our modern speech tries to describe the secret of their power. The writers of the New Testament described it more simply as the Spirit of God. In the last resort, they and we mean the same thing.

[1] Rom. v. 1-5.

CHAPTER VIII

THE WORD-OF-GOD SERVICE

PRAYER

A. PRAYER *FOLLOWED* THE READING AND PREACHING.

THIS appears to have been the invariable order in early worship. It was the order inherited from the synagogue ; and Justin's Sunday Service makes it appear that, up to the middle of the second century, the traditional order still held sway. And we can understand how congenial this order would be to a worship that was Spirit-controlled. All true Christian prayer, and not merely prayer of the ecstatic type, had to be inspired by the Spirit. Paul maintains that a man cannot even say that *Jesus is Lord* apart from the Spirit.[1] He attributes the consciousness of Sonship, which is indispensable to prayer, to the working of the Spirit.[2] These are cited as two of his briefer indications that the whole Christian life, inclusive of its life of prayer, was sustained and directed by the Spirit of God. Consequently, prayer was fittingly deferred till the proper atmosphere had been prepared for it through the reading and preaching of the Word of God. Luther gets to the heart of the matter :

" When the people are not first instructed by God, it is impossible to pray. Indeed, no one can pray aright by himself unless he preaches to himself beforehand. Through such preaching to oneself, the heart is moved and wakened to prayer. This is what happens in our churches. The voice of the holy preacher rings forth that the people may be instructed

[1] I Cor. xii. 3. [2] Gal. iv. 6.

in God's will.   After such preaching comes the prayer and thanksgiving." [1]

Heiler, who is one of our foremost authorities on Prayer, maintains firmly that prayer held this dominant place in the early Church.   If we except the celebration of the Lord's Supper, prayer was the culminating point of the worship, being led up to by the reading and preaching of the Word.

Very illuminating in this connection is the manner in which Clement closes his letter to the church at Corinth with his famous *Prayer*, which is the earliest complete prayer of the Christian Church that we possess apart from the short eucharistic prayers of the *Didachê*. Through fifty-eight chapters, Clement has been addressing all manner of earnest exhortation to his readers ; then in the fifty-ninth chapter he draws to a close, in this fashion :

> " But if some be disobedient to the words which have been spoken by God through us, let them know that they will entangle themselves in transgressions and no little danger ; but we shall be innocent of this sin, and will pray with eager entreaty and supplication that the Creator of the Universe may guard unhurt the number of his elect that has been numbered in all the world through his beloved child Jesus Christ, through whom he called us from darkness to light, from ignorance to the full knowledge of the glory of his name.   [Grant us] to hope in thy name, thou source of all creation ; open the eyes of our heart to know thee, that thou alone art the highest in the highest and remainest holy among the holy.   Thou dost humble the pride of the haughty, thou dost destroy the imaginings of nations, thou dost raise up the humble and abase the lofty, thou makest rich and makest poor, thou dost slay and make alive, thou alone art the finder of spirits and the God of all flesh, thou dost look on the abysses, thou seest into the works

[1] Quoted by Heiler, *Das Gebet*, p. 433.

of man, thou art the helper of those in danger, the saviour of those in despair, the creator and watcher over every spirit ; thou dost multiply nations upon earth and hast chosen out from them all those that love thee through Jesus Christ thy beloved child, and through him hast thou taught us, made us holy, and brought us to honour." [1]

The prayer then moves on, passing from ascriptions of praise to intercession for the afflicted, then back again to praise, followed by petition for forgiveness and for upholding in the ways of right and concord, and finally closing with intercession for secular rulers and governors.

What we notice, meantime, is the almost imperceptible transition from exhortation directed to man into prayer directed to God, and, more particularly, the exalted mood in which this transition is made. In the first sentence quoted, we see Clement possessed with the awareness of being the mouthpiece of God. His spirit mounts higher when he speaks of the eager entreaty and supplication he will address to God on his readers' behalf ; higher still, at thought of God's beloved Child and what He has done for all ; then, at this point, he glides with apparent ease and naturalness into his prayer. At the transition-point, there is sufficient irregularity in the Greek to give colour to the hypothesis that the prayer which follows was simply borrowed from the worship of his church at Rome. But no one who reads this transition-passage with the sympathy which good literature has a right to claim will find it easy to believe that Clement, when he began to write this passage, had already determined to add a borrowed prayer at the end, and was consciously working up to his quotation. Nor will a preacher, who has had the experience of passing from preaching to prayer without any sense of strain or effort, or even of readjustment, have difficulty in understanding Clement here. Quite patently, he is deeply moved as his letter draws to a close. His

[1] Translated by Lake, *The Apostolic Fathers* (Loeb Class. Liby.).

spirit kindles, more and more, till at last he finds himself speaking to God. And once begun to pray, he is swept on, along avenues of prayer he has often frequented when leading the worship in his Roman church ; falling back upon familiar thought-sequences, and upon phrases already well-tested and proven ; and yet giving forth no mere reproduction of past fervours, but a fresh and living prayer, fused into a unity of its own by the eagerness of his desire to help these troubled and dissident Corinthians. We owe Clement a large debt. Much of his letter, it must be confessed, is pedestrian stuff and confirms the sure instinct of the Church in excluding it from the Canon. But Clement can rise above his normal level, and does so rise at the end of his letter, where he not only gives us our first priceless example of the kind of prayer customary in the Christian worship of his day, but also, by revealing his own processes of mind and spirit, throws light upon the spiritual basis of the order of worship which prescribed that prayer should not precede, but should follow the reading and preaching of the Word.

Clement's prayer has other features which may confidently be regarded as typical of early Christian public prayer.

(a) Its *dependence upon Jewish literature and worship* is manifest. In the section of the prayer quoted above, there are no fewer than fourteen phrases, or clauses, which clearly derive from Jewish sources, either from the Old Testament or from the later Jewish writings or from the worship of the synagogue ; [1] while, on the other hand, there are strikingly few echoes of the New Testament. It is probable that in Clement's prayer the Jewish elements bulk larger than would be the case in the prayers of the earlier Church, since by his time the Enthusiasm was cooling and, though far from extinct, had lost its creative vigour and initiative. Still, it is the general opinion that, apart from the eucharistic prayers which were largely

[1] Von der Goltz, *op. cit.* p. 198.

centred upon Christ himself, the early Christian worship made free use of the Jewish stores of liturgical thought and language that were familiar and precious to the Church.

(b) It is a typical *free* prayer, simple and direct, sure and confident, fresh and vital, issuing—*de pectore*—from a warm and glowing spirit, which, while making use of modes of thought and phrase already in some degree fixed and stereotyped, fuses them afresh and pours them into moulds suited to the purpose of the hour. Nor is there any of that conscious elaboration of epithets or that piling up of synonyms which give to some of the prayers in later Eastern Liturgies the appearance less of prayers than of edifying discourses. In short, it is a prayer free from the restraints of rigid forms and from the encumbrance of labouring thought ; because it still moves in obedience to a mind and heart which are kindled by the Spirit of God.

(c) It is a typical prayer for use in *public worship*. It voices the aspirations and needs, not of an individual, nor of a class, but of a whole worshipping community. Everything that is particular, or individual, or accidental is suppressed ; only what is universal and common to all finds expression. So marked is this feature that although it is a fairly long prayer that would take more than five minutes to deliver, yet there is not a sentence in it, nor scarcely any phrase that could not be used in our own worship and trusted to evoke a response from the average worshipper of this modern age. And this is a remarkable thing. We are not surprised to find prayers of this universal type in the worship of the Roman Catholic Church, or in evangelical Liturgies which have been the products of long centuries of prayer-experience in communities embracing wide differences of social stratum, and culture, and temperament, and even of race. As Guardini says in the opening chapter of his little book, *Vom Geist der Liturgie.*

" These conditions (*for the growth of a Liturgy that will make a universal appeal*) emerge most clearly

when the devotional life of a great fellowship has been
able to develop through long periods."

The long periods he is thinking of comprise centuries.
Yet here, in Clement's prayer, we find universality attained
in little more than half a century. This is an index of the
rapidity of the Church's development in her early days, as
also of the strong spirit of fellowship that must have
prevailed, to be able thus to restrain, and finally to suppress
the voicing of mere individual experience, and that, too,
in communities where individual experience was intense
and must have striven for expression. It is a significant
achievement of first-century Worship that it should have
been able to produce a man like Clement, who, though
apparently no extraordinary man, was yet capable, when
he turned to public prayer, of giving forth a noble and
sustained utterance, in which we hear not so much his
own voice as the voice of the whole praying community
of his church.

B. IN PUBLIC WORSHIP, PRAYER WAS ADDRESSED TO GOD, NOT TO CHRIST.

(1) There is no evidence of prayers in public worship
having been addressed to Christ, during New Testament
times. Bousset [1] acknowledges this, although his conception of the early worship as a vigorous *Kyrioskult*
would welcome with open arms any indication of prayer
to Christ. We do not find such prayers till we reach the
Apocryphal Acts, which reflect popular Christianity about
the end of the second century and later : in these, the
address of prayer to Christ is frequent. Origen [2] combats
the practice, and in a tone which suggests that the practice
was common enough in his day to constitute a grave
problem. As we shall presently see, the attitude of the
earliest Church towards Christ was one of religious dependence and adoration, scarcely, if at all, to be dis-

---

[1] *Kyrios Christos* (1913), 102, 285.
[2] *Concerning Prayer,* 15, 16.

tinguished from the attitude of prayer ; and the fact that, in spite of this, prayer continued to be directed only to God is indicative of the strength residing in the mono-theistic tradition, and in the example of the Lord's Prayer, and in the apocalyptic habit of thought which presented the whole work of Salvation in the form of a purpose or plan of God—a form, that is to say, which in clear and vivid fashion placed in God's hands the supreme initiation and execution of that work and assigned to Christ the subordinate function of an executive agent.

(2) But while Origen combats the practice of addressing prayer to Christ, he also maintains that no prayer can be truly Christian which does not contain *some reference to Christ as our High-priest and Advocate with the Father*. Here, again, Origen reflects the practice of the early worship. Every complete prayer that we know of contains some direct reference to Christ, introduced in no incidental way, but in a fashion which shows that such reference was felt to be vital and essential. The prayer in the fourth chapter of *Acts*,[1] Clement's prayer, the eucharistic prayers of the *Didachê* and the prayer of the martyr Polycarp are evidence of the custom of praying to God *through thy (holy) child Jesus*. The Johannine and Ignatian Writings show that the form customary in their circles was prayer to the Father *in the name of Jesus Christ*. In whatever form the reference to Christ was made, it reflected the Church's belief in him as Mediator and Advocate with God.

(3) Although the regular prayers in worship were never addressed to Christ, *short ejaculatory petitions* were some-times directed to Him. Such were the prayer of the dying Stephen, " Lord Jesus, receive my spirit," and Paul's prayers concerning his thorn in the flesh, " I besought the Lord thrice." These were personal, individual prayers ; but in the " Maranatha," " Come, Lord Jesus," we have an apparent example of a public ejaculatory prayer to Christ, voicing the tense apocalyptic longing. It may well have happened in the worship-assemblies when men were

[1] 24–30.

strongly moved by the Spirit that short ejaculatory prayers to Christ were drawn from their lips. " He who prays in the name of Jesus, and with Jesus, will sooner or later pray to Jesus himself." But perhaps the most significant fact emerges in connection with Praise. There can be no question that many early Christian *hymns* were addressed to Christ himself. *Ephesians* [1] speaks explicitly of " singing and making melody in your heart to the Lord." In the *Apocalypse*,[2] the *new song* of the heavenly worship is addressed to Christ. Pliny's account of the " songs of praise sung to Christ as to a divinity," shows the custom to have been widespread.[3] This address of songs of praise direct to Christ is a fact of deep significance.

To sum up. While, on the one hand, prayers in public worship continued to be directed to God and not to Christ, on the other hand, the name of Christ appeared, significantly, in every prayer ; short ejaculatory petitions, often voicing a personal need, were directed to Him ; and, finally, hymns of praise were sung to Him. This indicates that while there was a reluctance in Worship to place Christ on an equality with God, yet He was worshipped and had divine honours paid to Him. It is for the systematic theologian to sift out the finer significances of these facts.

C. THE CONTENT OF THE PRAYERS.

We will survey the content of the prayers under the three headings of *Praise and Thanksgiving, Confession of Sin, Petition and Intercession.* Ever since Origen made his systematic study of Prayer, these have been the recognised component elements of a complete Christian prayer, and it is certain that they were all present in the Church's worship from the first. For convenience sake, the Doxology is reserved for treatment in the next chapter,

---

[1] v. 19.   [2] v. 9 f.

[3] Justin, *Trypho*, 63, 14 ff., says that *Psalm xlv.* was interpreted Christologically and sung to Christ.

although it might have been treated as a specialised form of the Praise of God.

The New Testament contains no example of a complete church prayer. On the other hand, there are many injunctions concerning Prayer, many echoes and perhaps actual fragments of church prayers, and also frequent snatches of personal prayer by Paul and others which cannot have differed vitally, in respect of their content, from the prayers in public worship. We will not aim at any close survey of these scattered details ; they have been assembled and studied in books which are easily accessible. We will be content with a brief estimate of the content of the prayers and, more particularly, of the relative preponderance of the various component elements mentioned above. It would be unhistorical to assume that Clement's prayer was typical, in this and other respects, of the prayers that went before it. Clement's prayer was the product of a time when the free initiative of Spirit-controlled worship was on the decline. The impulses of the Spirit were towards spontaneity and freedom and direct simplicity. Accordingly it is most probable that at first there was less divergence in form and content between private and public prayer than was the case later. Hence it is unlikely that such complete and comprehensive prayers as Clement's would be common in the earlier period ; probably it often happened that a prayer confined itself mainly to one or other of the component elements we have mentioned, in accordance with the prevailing mood of the worship at the moment. We need not, therefore, look for definite findings either as to the content of the early prayers or as to the order in which these contents were arranged.

(1) *Praise and Thanksgiving.*

We take these two elements together because we find that in practice they were not kept separate, and even in thought they can scarcely be held apart. Thus in Clement's prayer we have not a single sentence of formal

7

thanksgiving, though thanksgiving is implicit in the many
sentences which ascribe glory and praise to God. In the
three eucharistic prayers of the *Didachê*, the exact reverse
is the case. In each of these the opening words are
" We give thanks to Thee," and within this formula, for
the most part, their praise of God is voiced.

It is almost beyond question that in early Christian
Prayer praise and thanks predominated. Neither confession of sin nor petition had, relatively, so large a place
as was accorded to them later, when the prevailing mood
of worship had grown less confident and sure, and the
prayer for forgiveness and for stablishing in the Christian
way came more to the front.

When we deal in Chapter XIII. with the eucharistic
prayers, we will investigate the deeper motives which lay
behind this pre-eminence of praise and thanks. Meantime we may note a few of the briefer evidences of the
emphasis that was laid upon these elements. The early
Worship in Jerusalem is described in *Acts* as a " praising of
God." [1] Ignatius, with whom the early enthusiasm lingers
on into its Indian summer, calls the worship-gathering a
" coming together for thanksgiving and praise." [2] The
prayers which Paul devotes to thanksgiving outnumber
those devoted to petition ; while an examination of these
thanksgivings [3] reveals the rich variety of occasion which
he found for giving thanks. Also, his steady insistence on
the duty of giving thanks, always and in everything, must
have borne fruit in the worship-habits of his churches.
Finally, we have the *a priori* consideration that the confident and joyous enthusiasm of that early period would
find more natural expression in praise and thanksgiving
than in confession and petition.

(2) *Confession of sin.*

At this point we are met by an almost total lack of
evidence bearing directly on the early worship ; so we

---

[1] ii. 46 f.   [2] *Eph.* xiii. 1.

[3] As tabulated by Von der Goltz, *op. cit.* 109 ff.

must seek our clues from Paul. Now, it is quite clear that
the intensive culture of sin-consciousness or of sin-con-
fession was never an aim of Paul's, neither for himself nor
for his churches. What he mainly sought to foster was
the conquering spirit of confidence and joy. His most
congenial line of admonition was this : " Regard yourselves
as dead to sin ; you are alive to God ; your sins are behind
you, forgiven ; therefore be thankful, thankful, thankful." [1]
This did not mean that he shut his eyes to the real truth
about his people ; no one could be more earnest or more
pointed in rebuking or warning against specific sins. But
he adopted this line only when it was urgently called for ;
while his normal appeals were to men's idealism and to
the impulses making for goodness and for confidence in
achieving it. It is therefore probable that the absence of
explicit and detailed confession of sin from his recorded
prayers is no accident, and that his churches, following
his example, did not as a rule go much beyond some simple
words of contrition combined with an earnest petition
for forgiveness.

In the later part of the century when the enthusiasm
was cooling, we should expect a less confident mood and
a keener sense of weakness and need. Thus, the *Didachê*
lays an emphasis upon Confession which is more marked
than anything we find in Paul. " In the congregation
thou shalt confess thy transgressions, and thou shalt not
betake thyself to prayer with an evil conscience." [2]   Again :
" Hold Eucharist after confessing your transgressions
that your offering may be pure." [3]   Clement introduces
Confession well on in his prayer, interlacing it with the
prayer for forgiveness.

> " O merciful and compassionate, forgive us our
> iniquities, and unrighteousness, and transgressions,
> and shortcomings. Reckon not every sin of thy

---

[1] Rom. vi. 11 ; Col. ii. 12–14, 20 : with i. 12, ii. 7, iii. 15 ff.,
iv. 2.

[2] iv. 14.   [3] xiv. 1.

servants and handmaids,[1] but cleanse us with the cleansing of thy truth, and guide our steps. . . ."

This is our first actual example of a prayer of confession, dating from the end of the century ; but even here we have a simplicity and conciseness which evince no effort at elaboration or special emphasis on confession.

It may be regarded as certain, however, that confession of sin was instinctively recognised from the first to be a necessary component of all true prayer. The *Didachê* may reveal a growing emphasis on this element of worship ; yet its warnings against betaking oneself to prayer and against making one's offering (of thanks and praise) at the Eucharist with a conscience uncleansed by confession issued from a true spiritual instinct which must have been alive from the first. Accordingly, we may regard the confession of sins and the request for forgiveness, however briefly expressed, as constants in all Christian prayer.

(3) *Petition* and *Intercession*.

We combine Petition and Intercession under one survey, because any clear line of demarcation between them would, for early Christian prayer, be somewhat arbitrary. The reason for this is that the petitions in New Testament worship were directed pre-eminently upon spiritual blessings; they were loyal to the Divine ideal, "seek ye first the Kingdom of God " ; their burden was the advancement of God's reign, whether in the individual, or in the local church, or in the Church as a whole. Moreover, the vivid sense of fellowship as members all of the one Body of Christ, and the resultant sense that the welfare or suffering of one involved the welfare or suffering of all, went far to soften those distinctions between *I* and *you* and *they* upon which any clear discrimination between Petition and Intercession must ultimately rest.

Paul's petitions are all for spiritual things ; for when he

[1] This reference to men and women is one of the clearer indications that Clement's prayer had its origins in the public worship of the community.

does pray for some boon of a more material kind, it is always bound up with his calling as a servant of Jesus Christ. For his readers and for the Church at large, his prayers are for such things as grace, peace, love, unity, and that they may be " kept unto the day of Jesus Christ." We have already mentioned the prayer for forgiveness as a constant in Petition. Constant also was petition for the welfare of the Church. The prayer summarised in the fourth chapter of *Acts* [1] may be accepted as reflecting an established habit of petition. It pleads for the success of the work of the Apostles, for protection against adversaries, for a confident proclaiming of the message, and for a demonstration with power of its effectiveness. The *Didachê* must echo an old fashion of petition :

" Remember, Lord, Thy Church, to deliver it from all evil and to make it perfect in Thy love, and gather it together in its holiness from the four winds to Thy kingdom which Thou hast prepared for it." [2]

" As this broken bread was scattered upon the mountains, but was brought together and became one, so let Thy Church be gathered together from the ends of the earth into Thy kingdom, for Thine is the glory and the power through Jesus Christ for ever." [3]

Ignatius and Polycarp both show how deeply rooted was this habit of prayer for the Church. There was prayer also for the Christian brother who had sinned or who had fallen away, although the writer of *1 John* discourages such prayer in the case of a sin which is " unto death." [4] It is not till we reach the *First Epistle to Timothy* [5] that we find an injunction that prayer should be offered for the world outside the Church ; we will return to this matter presently. Clement's prayer gives us our first example of such wider petitions. Noteworthy here is the balanced and finished choice of thought and expression.

[1] 24–30.   [2] x. 5.   [3] ix. 4.
[4] v. 16.   [5] ii. 1.

> " And to our rulers, Lord, grant health, peace,
> concord, firmness, that they may administer the
> government which Thou hast given them without
> offence."

This is at once a petition that Christians may be loyally
obedient to their heathen rulers and that these rulers
should be withheld from persecution and oppression of the
Church.[1] Noteworthy also is the absence here of any
petition that these rulers may be brought to a knowledge
of the truth and become Christian. That was a thought
that lay beyond the horizon even of the second century.
The earthly kingdom and the Kingdom of God stood in
stark opposition ; the earthly kingdom could not be
without its Emperor, but a Christian an Emperor could
never be.[2] Finally, we have Clement's comprehensive
prayer for

> " those of us who are in affliction ; have mercy on the
> lowly, raise the fallen, show Thyself to those in need,
> heal the sick, turn again the wanderers of Thy people,
> feed the hungry, ransom our prisoners, raise up the
> weak, comfort the faint-hearted, let all nations know
> Thee that Thou art God alone, and that Jesus Christ
> is Thy Child, and that we are Thy people and the
> sheep of Thy pasture."

In connection with Petition and Intercession, two
matters call for more special attention.

(a) The first is the almost complete lack of New Testament evidence for prayer having been offered on behalf
of the great world outside the Church. In the undoubted
epistles of Paul there is no reference to such prayer ; the

---

[1] Cf. Rom. xiii. 1 ; 1 Pet. ii. 13 ff.

[2] Tertullian, *Apology*, xxi. " Sed et Caesares credidissent super
Christo, si aut Caesares non essent saeculo necessarii, aut si et
Christiani potuissent esse Caesares."

one exception is Paul's praying for his own beloved people.[1]
It is not until we reach that apparently late writing which
we know as *I Timothy* that we find such prayer enjoined.
" My first counsel is that supplications, prayers, petitions,
and thanksgivings are to be offered for all men—for kings
and all in authority . . . "[2]

In view of the frequency and variety of the New Testament references to prayer, it is unlikely that its silence
on the universal range of prayer was merely an accident.
Moffatt[3] stresses the fact that the thought of God as the
Father of men, *qua* men, was not a vital and operative
thought in the New Testament ; God was the Father, in
an effective sense, only of His own redeemed sons.   What
we have, therefore, is a radical differentiation of mankind
into two classes in respect of their nearness to God ; and
alongside of this a constant effort to keep Christian love
practical, and a refusal to substitute for its practical
energies some mere sentiment of universal goodwill.
The primary sphere for the exercise of this love was the
Christian brotherhood, while outside and around it lay
the world, the sphere of evil and of varied antagonisms
to the Church.   Accordingly, it was neither unnatural
nor unwholesome if, with such a background of thought
and experience, the first Christians did not pour out
petitions to God indiscriminately on behalf of all, but
directed them towards the urgent needs that called to
them from within their own fellowship.   It may have been
that in their overpowering sense of the joys and privileges
that were theirs as members of the household of God they
drew the line between themselves and " those outside "
with an undue sharpness.   It may even have been that
they conceived of the world outside as being a sphere
where the prayer-forces that operated with such rich
result within the brotherhood ceased somehow to be
effective.   Such conceptions would betoken a certain
narrowing of thought.   On the other hand, we know,

[1] Rom. x. 1.   [2] ii. 1 f.
[3] *Love in the New Testament*, p. 70.

from the *Epistle to Timothy*, that they quickly emancipated themselves from these limiting ideas, if indeed they ever entertained them ; and we further know—and this is the important thing—that never at any time was there a narrowing of their *sympathies* with those who were outside. They never were lacking either in desire or in effort to share with the heathen world the privileges and the blessings of their fellowship. After all, the greatest service that the Church can ever render to the world is to preach the Gospel to it. The message which Jesus sent to John the Baptist and which culminated in the re-minder that the poor had the Gospel preached to them [1] was no anticlimax ; nor was its meaning lost upon the early Church. If it did not pray for the heathen world outside, it spent itself to the utmost carrying the Gospel to it. What better could it have done ?

(*b*) To what extent, and in what spirit was the help of prayer enlisted in dealing with individual necessities, for example, with the needs of the sick ?

Of such use of prayer we have various records in the New Testament, while in the succeeding literature they become more frequent. *Acts* tells of the raising of Tabitha by Peter, after prayer ; [2] also of the healing of the father of Publius by Paul, through prayer and the laying-on of hands ; [3] while *James* gives directions regarding the anointing of the sick with oil, accompanied with prayer. [4] These and other references in the New Testament and in the subsequent writings—notably Tertullian's account of the manifold effects of prayer [5]—demonstrate a profound belief in the efficacy of prayer for meeting certain types of individual need. Our modern minds are apt to shy at the Church's accounts of her wonders and healings ; and, finding some traces of legend or superstition, we incline to shelve the whole question for the time being. Yet we must reckon with the fact that Paul, in his list of the gifts of the Spirit, sets down gifts of *miracle-working* and of

[1] Matt. xi. 5.   [2] ix. 40.   [3] xxviii. 8.
[4] v. 14 f.   [5] *De Oratione*, 29.

healing ; [1] and not only so, but he speaks of these with an air of assurance and of almost matter-of-fact calmness which demonstrates, beyond a shadow of doubt, that for him and his readers such things belonged to the category of the familiar and the unquestioned. Even a scholar so modern in mind as Johannes Weiss describes these facts as " facts of the utmost historical significance." [2] Writing on a later occasion to the same people, Paul says : " You had all the miracles that mark an Apostle done for you fully and patiently—miracles, wonders, and deeds of power." [3] Here he claims to have wrought these deeds of power himself. Since it is almost certain that such deeds of power would usually be preceded by a prayer that the power of God might be released for action, we seem shut up to the conclusion that such prayer was far from rare in New Testament times. In many cases it would be offered in private beside the sick-bed; but there can be little doubt that it would sometimes happen that sufferers were brought to the worship-gathering, and that there, in its intimate and informal atmosphere, the prayer and the healing were carried through. The passage quoted from *II Corinthians* almost seems to suggest that it had happened so at Corinth. Of one thing we may feel certain, that all prayers offered thus on behalf of the sick were charged with the conviction that they really availed towards securing their end. It has been alleged that, even during the first century, prayer was commonly employed as a magic influence or formula ; but of this there is no clear evidence. No doubt some of the Gentile converts would tend to regard prayer in this magic light. But if the Johannine writings may be taken as reflecting the mind of the Church in general towards the close of the century, we gather from them that while the word of the Johannine Christ, " Whatsoever ye shall ask in my name that will I do," was accepted at its full value, the attached reservation was also held firmly in mind that what was sought must be in

[1] I Cor. xii. 28.   [2] *Commentary on I Cor.* xii. 9.
[3] 2 Cor. xii. 12 ; cf. Rom. xv. 19.

harmony with the will of God.[1]   The purpose of prayer
was to get God's will done on earth ; it was not as yet
being employed as a lever for getting man's will done in
Heaven.

[1] 1 John v. 14.

CHAPTER IX

THE WORD-OF-GOD SERVICE

PRAYER (*continued*). PRAISE

IN connection with Prayer, three matters remain for consideration. These are: The Doxology; The Amen; The Lord's Prayer in Worship.

(a) The Doxology.

In the Jewish worship of the Synagogue, the Doxology was an adjunct to every prayer, and the practice appears to have been consistently followed in the Christian worship.[1] Both in form and substance, the Jewish model was closely copied. The simplest form seems to have been, *To Thee be glory for ever.* In various ways this was expanded in the Christian worship; but these expansions, or additions, do not pass beyond the limits of Jewish thought and expression, except in one vital particular to be mentioned presently. The variety of the New Testament forms of the Doxology is indicative of the freedom which prevailed. The doxologies are composed in the rhythmical prose which is familiar in exalted prayer and hymn; and while they retain their freedom to select the most worthy ascriptions of praise and glory that the Spirit-impulse may suggest, they never yield to the weakness of extravagance or redundancy, but remain strong, dignified, and reverential.

The distinctively Christian element is the incorporation of some reference to Christ. Occasionally this might be merely implicit—in the designation of God as *Father*; but was usually explicit, " through Jesus Christ ": " To the only wise God be glory through Jesus Christ for ever and

[1] For detail of the various forms of the Doxology in the New Testament, see Chase, *The Lord's Prayer in the Early Church.*

ever." [1] We have already noted the significance of this practice of introducing the name of Christ into these solemn ascriptions of praise and glory. The doxology is addressed to God, except in one case,[2] where it is directed to Christ alone. The address to Christ is not frequent in the sub-apostolic age. The Trinitarian form emerges for the first time in the prayer of Polycarp : " Jesus Christ, through whom, to Thee, with Him and the Holy Ghost, be glory. . . ." In the second century, the triple ascription becomes frequent ; in the third, customary.

The steadfast adherence to the Jewish custom of closing each prayer with a sonorous ascription of praise and glory to God must have exercised a strong influence on Christian Prayer. The old Jewish spirit of reverential homage and awe before the Majesty of God found clear and constant expression in these closing phrases of every Christian Prayer. Anything incongruous, or extravagant, or trivial in the prayer itself was exposed and rebuked by the exalted words at the end, which must therefore have acted as a constant restraint upon all forms of excess. If we may say so, the Spirit did, at this point, welcome and admit a definite form-barrier against the abuse of prayer. It was as though the old Religion had bequeathed to the new a model which bodied forth what was highest in her own worship of God—a model, at once so expressive that any one could appreciate it and so compact that he could easily handle it, while subconsciously employing it as a standard by which to measure his speech and bearing when he stood in the presence of the Highest.

(b) The Amen.

From the first, in accordance with Jewish custom, the Amen was spoken by the worshipping people.[3] The earliest instance of the Amen being spoken by the man who utters the prayer is found in Polycarp's prayer, where the presence

---

[1] Rom. xvi. 27.
[2] 2 Pet. iii. 18; Heb. xiii. 21 and 1 Pet. iv. 11 are doubtful cases.
[3] 1 Cor. xiv. 16 ; Rev. v. 14, vii. 12 ; Justin, *Apology*, i. 65. 3.

of a worshipping community cannot be presupposed. Thereafter, the original significance of the *Amen* was frequently lost sight of, and it was used, both in public and private prayer, as a simple reinforcement of the prayer, or as an expression of confidence that it would be answered.

But at first, the *Amen* was invariably a response, spoken by the worshipping people. It implied that they assented to what had been said, and that they appropriated it as their own. They identified themselves with the Leader's prayer, and solemnly confessed the inner unity which bound him and them together. In this single closing word, therefore, there came to expression one fundamental quality of Christian prayer. It was *community-prayer*. It was not the prayer of a priest or an individual speaking on behalf of others. It was more even than the sum of a number of individual prayers ascending to God. It was, in some way, a real collective prayer, spoken by a company which approached God collectively as the Body of Christ, voicing, " with one accord," the great experiences they shared together. Later, the conception was visualised in the praying figure of the *Ecclesia orans* of the Catacombs.

This raises questions both for the historian of Religions and for the psychologist. To the former it presents the problem of the extent to which this collective consciousness in Christian worship was a survival of the collectivism that was native to ancient thought, and was deeply ingrained in the old tribal thinking of the Jews. For the psychologist the question of crowd-psychology emerges. This latter question is ventilated by R. S. Simpson in one of the most sympathetic studies of Worship that Presbyterian thought has produced.[1] The quotations which follow are from his work.

" Modern psychology emphasises this, that when you come to what one may call a very high group of

[1] *Ideas in Corporate Worship.*—It will always be a matter of profound regret that Dr. Simpson was not spared to annotate and complete his work.

individuals, that is, a group which is more than an accidental crowd, a group of men which is possessed by a real intellectual or spiritual interest, then the more clearly shall you find that something spiritual or psychical is added by the group to that which is contributed by the individual members of the group. I mean, there appears an idea in the group which is not in the individual mind of the members of the group. There come to be subtly and mysteriously blended in the group, traditions, memories, suggestions, the poetry of an ideal and the stored riches of a continued life ; and these from the group act upon the individual members who compose the group, so that in a very especial sense something new is added by the group consciousness to the consciousness of each individual who has a part within it. Now this applies in a very real sense to a worshipping congregation of Christian people. There is something added to the individual as he worships, not by himself, but in fellowship with others. Modern psychology is quite clear about that."

" In the especial matter of worship there is a definite promise to the group which is quite distinct from the promise of the presence to the individual. ' Where two or three are gathered together in my name, I am in the midst.' "

" Psychology teaches that something of great importance is added to the individual when he associates himself in worship with a group " (pp. 47–49).

(c) The Lord's Prayer in Worship.

To what extent was the Lord's Prayer used in Worship ? For the New Testament period, no satisfactory answer can be given. The accounts, in *Matthew* and *Luke*, of our Lord's teaching his disciples to pray do not prove that he intended his model prayer to be more than an example of

the fitting content and of the right spirit of prayer.   Indeed,
the variations in the wording of the three forms that have
reached us (in *Matthew, Luke*, and the *Didachê*) point to
its not having been taught as a fixed formulary of prayer ;
for while these variations indicate a knowledge and use
of the prayer in various localities, they disclose also the
absence of anxious care to preserve the exact wording
of the original form.   Another important fact is this :
beyond the two passages referred to, there is no undisputed
reference in the New Testament to the Prayer.   All this
suggests that the use of the Prayer in worship was not so
general in our period as it became later.   This can be
understood.   While the Enthusiasm lasted and prayer
remained a living, spontaneous thing, no need would be
felt for any fixed form.   On the other hand, we must keep
in view the probability that, even in the free worship,
individuals might often feel moved to pray in the familiar
and sacred words.

We have to distinguish between a *liturgical* and a *private*
use of the Prayer.   The Jewish hours of prayer—morning,
afternoon, and sunset—were probably widely adopted for
private Christian prayer.   Now, the individual would not
be able to depend on himself for a free and Spirit-inspired
prayer on all these stated occasions.   Consequently, some
more or less fixed private ritual, or form of prayer, must
have been common.   In such circumstances, the Lord's
Prayer would offer itself as containing words of the highest
inspiration.   It is probable that when the *Didachê*,[1] after
setting down the Lord's Prayer, adds, "pray thus three
times a day," it is enjoining a private and not a liturgical
use of the Prayer.

While, therefore, a private use of the Prayer is highly
probable during the first century, there is no clear evidence
of a regular, stated use in public worship.   Nor do the
a priori probabilities favour it.   The first mention of the
Prayer as incorporated in a Liturgy comes from Cyril of
Jerusalem (*c.* A.D. 348).

[1] Chapter viii.

PRAISE—*Psalms and Hymns*

A few fragmentary remains, scattered over the New Testament, are almost all that we possess of the distinctively Christian hymns of the early worship. Nor has any one of the sacred writers paused to indicate the form and content of these hymns, or the manner in which they were sung. Consequently we have to rely upon such inferences as may be drawn from sparse and incidental hints. Indeed, our difficulties are actually greater than usual, by reason of the fact that we get scarcely any assistance from the writers of the second century, or even those of the third century, and so must depend on the New Testament itself for our knowledge of the early Praise in a more exclusive measure than in the case of her Prayers and Sacraments. There are substantial reasons for this silence on the part of the records, both earlier and later ; but we shall be in a better position to appreciate these reasons a few pages farther on.

A priori, we should expect that a movement which released so much emotion, and loyalty, and enthusiasm, would find expression in Song. This proved to be the case in after ages when the religion was already grown old and had need to rediscover some of the truth she had forgotten or mislaid ; notably in the revivals associated with Protestantism and Wesleyan Methodism, the return of the light was hailed with wonderful outbursts of song. So it would have been strange indeed if the Church had remained songless in that first glorious dawn when the light from Christ came breaking across the horizons, making all things new. Nor was the singing of praise to God a strange or unpractised art for the Christians of the first generation. Behind them lay an ancient habit of Praise. From temple and from synagogue the strains of the Psalms had been rising to God for generations. It has to be admitted that our knowledge of synagogue practice in the early Christian era is shrouded in uncertainties ; but while it is probable that in the synagogues of the motherland the singing of praise was a slower development, it is equally probable that in the less conservative Greek-speaking synagogues dispersed throughout the Gentile world this development had already matured before the coming of Christ.[1]

A few of the psalms, or hymns, preserved in the New Testament are more Jewish than Christian. In the opening chapters of *Luke* [2] we find three such Jewish songs of praise—those of Mary, Zacharias, and Simeon—all modelled, both in form and content, on the pattern of the Old Testament. Again, in the Book of *Revelation*, we find quite a number [3] of songs of praise. Some of these [4] are manifestly Christian creations—*new songs*—such as could not have been sung in an earlier time; but others are as clearly not new but old, with no word or phrase that might not have been used by a Jewish worshipper of the century before Christ. It would be unwise to claim these latter as Christian hymns; it is more natural to regard them as borrowed from the familiar worship of the Greek - speaking synagogue.

It is probable that from very early times the Church used as her Praise-book the *Psalms of David*—these Psalms, like the rest of the Old Testament, having been appropriated as a specifically Christian possession. But inevitably they were inadequate, by themselves, to express the deepening and expanding experience of the Church; and though we would gladly know more regarding the use that was made of them, it is of greater moment to inquire into the beginnings of a Psalmody and Hymnody that were distinctively Christian.[5]

[1] Lietzmann, *Geschichte der alten Kirche*, i. 151 f.
[2] i. 46–55, 68–79, ii. 29–32.
[3] i. 4–7, v. 9–14, xii. 10–12, xix. 1 f., 5–8, xxi. 3 f.
iv. 8, iv. 11, xv. 3 f., xi. 15–18, vii. 12.
[4] The first five.
[5] Lest there be confusion about terms, it should be noted that *psalm, hymn,* and *spiritual song* appear to have been used by the early Church as practically synonymous terms. Since Jerome's day,

8

When Paul says : [1] " When you meet together, each contributes something—a song of praise, a lesson, a revelation,
a ' tongue,' an interpretation," it is generally agreed that
by a *song of praise* he meant, not an Old Testament psalm,
but some new Christian song.   Again, when he and Silas
" sang praises unto God " in prison at midnight,[2] probably
these were Christian songs improvised under the tense
experience of the moment.   From Pliny's *Letter to Trajan*
we learn that in the province of Bithynia it was a regular
custom, in the Christian worship of that time (*c.* A.D. 112),
to " sing to Christ as to a divinity " ; and further that
this singing was " antiphonal." [3]   This latter point need
occasion no surprise, since antiphonal singing was not
only an ancient tradition of the Greek drama, but " had
been practised with much elaboration of detail in the
psalmody of the Jews, as appears from the account which
Philo gives of the Egyptian Therapeutes," [4] and so its
introduction into the Christian Church was a matter of
course almost from the beginning.   Probably the new
song [5] of the heavenly worship in the Book of *Revelation*
is an echo of the antiphonal praise practised in the
Church.

> " Thou art worthy
>> to take the book, and to open the seals thereof ;
>> for thou wast slain,
>> and hast redeemed us to God by thy blood,

persistent efforts have been made to differentiate them as they
appear together in Col. iii. 16 and Eph. v. 19 ; but most scholars now
think that Paul had no clear distinction in mind when he wrote.
Psalm and *hymn* were the more religious words, *song* being more
colourless and so requiring an ancillary adjective.   In the first three
Christian centuries, there seems a distinct reluctance to use the
word *hymn*, probably because that was the current term for heathen
cult-songs.   Perhaps *new songs* was the only distinctive term which
lay at hand to designate the new productions.

[1] 1 Cor. xiv. 26.   [2] Acts xvi. 25.
[3] See Appendix A.   [4] Lightfoot, *Apostolic Fathers*, ii. 1, p. 31.
[5] v. 8–14.

out of every kindred, and tongue, and people,
   and nation ;
and hast made us unto our God kings and priests :
and we shall reign on the earth."

That is the *new song*, sung to Christ by the four beasts
and the four-and-twenty elders. The burden of the song
is then taken up and repeated by the whole angelic chorus
of heaven, " ten thousand times ten thousand, and
thousands of thousands " :

" Worthy is the Lamb that was slain
      to receive power, and riches, and wisdom,
      and strength, and honour, and glory, and
         blessing."

Next follows the doxology, or ascription of praise, uttered
in chorus by the whole multitude of the lower creatures
of earth and sky :

" Blessing, and honour, and glory, and power,
   unto Him that sitteth upon the throne,
   and unto the Lamb, for ever and ever."

Finally, the *Amen*, spoken by the four beasts.

There is a passage in *Colossians* [1] which suggests, very
strongly, that the stream of song which flowed through
the early worship was a considerable one. Paul wrote as
follows :

" And you must be thankful. Let the inspiration
of Christ dwell in your midst with all its wealth of
wisdom ; teach and train one another with the music
of psalms, with hymns, and songs of the spiritual life ;
praise God with thankful hearts. Indeed, whatever
you say and do, let everything be done in dependence
on the Lord Jesus, giving thanks in his name to God
the Father."

Now there is in this no faintest hint of there being
anything out of the common in the injunction to " teach

[1] iii. 16.

and train one another with the music of psalms, with hymns, and songs of the spiritual life." The passage suggests, rather, that Paul is simply underlining a practice which he knew to be already established, with a view to its encouragement. The thought dominating the whole passage is that of gratitude and thanksgiving to God ; and the singing of psalms, and hymns, and spiritual songs comes into Paul's mind, as he writes, simply as being one of the most natural and effective ways in which such gratitude could find expression and reinforcement. In these early worship-gatherings that were so vitally quickened by the Spirit, or, as it is put here, by the " word " or " inspiration " of Christ, it must often have happened that a worshipper would rise and pour himself out in praises of Christ, making use of that solemn rhythmical prose in which the religious praise of that age, and of the ages before it, found its most common outlet, and a few examples of which we shall presently be examining. Many of these first Christian praises would have small literary value. Improvisations of the moment, they would serve to express the quickened emotion of the speaker and to stir responsive chords in like-quickened worshippers about him ; yet they would quickly be forgotten as soon as some new interest swept the meeting.[1] But occasionally there would be produced something worthy of a longer life ; and this would arrest the attention, and would fix itself in the memory of this man or of that, who might give utterance to it again on some later occasion, and perhaps in some richer and more artistic form. Thus it would go on passing from mind to mind, till at length it became widely familiar, and established for itself a place in the currency of Christian diction and thought. Happily there have been preserved in the New Testament a few examples of the more finished products of the early Praise, and some of these

---

[1] The *spirituals* given forth at negro camp-meetings are adduced as a parallel, by E. F. Scott, *Moffatt, New Testament Commentary* in loco.

may have been chiselled into their present shape in the
course of some such process as we have just described.
We will examine three of the more outstanding.

(1) *Ephesians* v. 14.

> " Awake, O sleeper,
>   and rise from the dead,
>   and Christ will shine upon you."

" We may regard this almost certainly as belonging to
an early Christian hymn, of which everything is now lost
except this beautiful verse." [1] It is the opinion of many
that the hymn was originally used in connection with
Baptism, as a song of welcome into the new life, as the
convert was rising again from the water : " Wake up,
O sleeper, and rise from the dead, and (hereafter) Christ
will shine upon you."

(2) *1 Timothy* iii. 16.

> He who was
> " manifested in flesh,
>   vindicated in spirit,
>   seen by angels,
>   preached among Gentiles,
>   believed on in the world,
>   taken up in glory."

The writer introduces this verse as a summary of the
profound and mysterious truth of our religion. For long
it has been recognised that his words are a quotation ;
but it is still debated whether they should be regarded as
a quotation from a hymn, or as a quotation from some
formula of Confession of faith. This opens out a most
interesting and important subject. Scholars are being
led to recognise that in the early worship there was a very
intimate connection between these three things, *Thanksgiving-prayer*, *Hymns*, and *Credal-confessions*. In all
three the style and diction employed were substantially

[1] E. F. Scott, *op. cit.*

the same. All alike were couched in a stately, rhythmical
prose ; the words were Greek, but the structure of the
sentences was Semitic and wholly un-Greek ; while the
style was solemn, exalted, hieratical.[1] When we come
to deal with the eucharistic prayers of thanksgiving,[2] we
will be in a better position to understand the deeper
motives conditioning this kinship between Prayer, Hymns,
and Credal-confessions. Meantime we observe that the
Hymns were not yet differentiated, in diction and style,
from the other two. They were not yet *metrical* structures,
in our sense of the word. It was not till about the time of
Augustine that hymns began to be composed in the
forms with which we are familiar.[3] Previous to that,
they adhered to the rhythmical prose which was
common throughout the religious worship of the
ancient East.

So the question with which we started, as to whether
this passage from *1 Timothy* is to be construed as a hymn or
as a credal formula, is not a very vital one. Possibly, by
the time of writing, it had attained the latter character :
but, if so, it must have had a previous history within the
worship, either as a hymn, or as a part of the gradually
evolving material of thanksgiving prayer ; since we have
strong reason for thinking that it was out of elements

[1] It is not possible, without quoting extensively from original
sources, to describe the features of this structure and style ; the task
has been accomplished by Norden in his pioneering book, *Agnostos
Theos* (1913). But its main qualities can be felt by a modern reader
even of the Authorised English Version ; and if he has an ear for
such things he must be aware of the essential poetry lying behind
the stately prose of such passages as *Philippians* ii. 6–11, or the
prayer-like opening paragraphs of *Colossians*, or the *new songs* of the
Apocalypse. We would have been spared much tribulation, if only
our fathers had been in a position to see that a passage like the so-
called *Kenosis-passage* (Phil. ii. 6–11) was first composed in the
mood and manner of an inspired poet, and, only in a very secondary
degree, in that of a scientific theologian.

[2] Chapter XIII.

[3] Probably under the influence of the new manner of praise
introduced by Ambrose.

which first took shape in Prayer or Hymn that the Credal
confessions were eventually developed.

(3) *Philippians* ii. 6–11.
  " Who being in the form of God,
    thought it not robbery
      to be equal with God ;

    but made himself of no reputation,
      taking upon him the form of a servant,
        and being made in the likeness of men ;

    and being found in fashion as a man,
      he humbled himself
        and became obedient unto death,
        even the death of the cross.

  WHEREFORE God also hath highly exalted him,
    and given him a name
      which is above every name ;

    that at the name of Jesus
      every knee should bow
        of things in heaven, and things in earth, and
              things under the earth ;

    and that every tongue should confess
      that Jesus Christ is Lord,
        to the glory of God the Father."

The arrangement in six stanzas, of three lines each, is
that adopted by Lohmeyer in his recent distinguished
Monograph on the passage.[1] In the original Greek, this
arrangement is even more convincing than in the English.
The lines are, with rare exceptions, triple-accented ; even
the concluding line of the second last stanza contains only
three accented words (it contains only five Greek words in

[1] *Kyrios Jesus*, 1928.

all, as against the thirteen in the English).[1] The first three stanzas describe the Humiliation ; the latter three the Exaltation ; and the whole is exactly divided between these two themes, the second being introduced by the emphatic *Wherefore*. There can be no question that we have here a highly-finished and exquisitely-balanced work of art ; and one so packed with thought that its two sentences suffice to unfold the mighty cosmic drama of Salvation. Lohmeyer is inclined to think that this hymn was not the work of Paul himself, but must have come from some Great Unknown, some poet-prophet of the earlier Church. He also thinks that Paul may have become acquainted with it through the Worship, where it may have established itself in the eucharistic prayers of some church. Although we may not be able to follow Lohmeyer in these surmises, we must at least feel that this great and finished poem cannot have flowed *extempore* from even Paul's pen, at the moment of his reaching this point in his letter to Philippi. In itself it is a complete unity ; its sweep of thought far transcends the immediate level and purpose of his writing ; and it bears every mark of being a previously complete and independent whole. Another great scholar—one of the most distinguished and reverent of our living authorities on the early worship, also designates this work as a *hymn*, and goes on to say that, should we attempt to visualise Paul conducting a eucharistic service in some one of his churches, we might not be far astray if we put into his mouth a eucharistic prayer that would unfold the greatness of Christ in some such fashion as this.[2]

Once more we are made sensible of the connection between eucharistic Prayer, Hymn, and Confession of faith ;

[1] The one drawback to this arrangement is that the words *even the death of the cross* are difficult to fit into it ; either they make the last line of the stanza rather long, or they add a fourth line to it. Lohmeyer, who thinks that the hymn was not composed by Paul, attributes to Paul the addition of these words, as being an irresistible comment for him to make.

[2] Lietzmann, *Messe und Herrenmahl*, p. 178 ff.

this great passage might quite well be conceived as functioning in any one of these capacities.

Why have so few early Christian hymns been preserved ?

(1) The scantiness of hymn-deposits in the literature is not exceptional ; the deposits from the worship as a whole are almost as fragmentary. The young Religion was too engrossed in living its life to take thought of keeping records of it. And there was no impulse to make records on behoof of after ages. There were to be no after ages ; the end of the world was at hand ; " the hammer of the world's clock was already raised to strike."

(2) The early hymns had nothing sufficiently distinctive to make them stand out from other elements of Worship so as to claim special attention. God and Christ were praised in traditional forms. There was no need to create new forms. Individual efforts in this direction may have been made, in imitation of Pagan models ; but it was not to be expected that any man of sufficient poetical genius would be at hand to create new forms of Christian Praise worthy of endurance. The great men of the Church were preoccupied with other things. Clement of Alexandria's hymn is the earliest in a new form that has been preserved.

(3) When we have regard to the working of the Spirit, and to the richness of the diction-material that lay at hand, it seems probable that most of the early hymns would be improvised. We can conceive the Spirit impelling to utterance in the rhythmical prose of the hymn, as readily as in the kindred diction of exalted prayer. Such improvisation of hymns appears to have been known as late as Tertullian, who challenges Marcion to point to gifts of his God that could be set alongside the Church's gifts : *edat aliquem psalmum, aliquam visionem, aliquam orationem, dumtaxat spiritualem, in ecstasi.* . . . Improvisation does not conduce to permanence.

(4) About the middle of the third century there was a strong orthodox reaction against the hymn-singing of the

day.[1] The Gnostics had made large use of hymns, framed so as to catch the popular taste ; and the Church, taking alarm, condemned all such hymns as too modern and worldly, and forbade the use of any hymns except such as were to be found in the Scriptures. This arrested the production of new hymns, and suppressed any of the less biblical type that might be in use. This " biblicising " movement lasted for a period, and the policy was surrendered only when the resultant impoverishment of the Church's Praise was realised. It is probable that many earlier hymns that might otherwise have been preserved passed into oblivion at this time.

[1] Kroll, *Die Christliche Hymnodik*, p. 38.

CHAPTER X

THE SACRAMENTS

THE LORD'S SUPPER [1]

THE earliest description of the manner of celebrating the Lord's Supper in the Christian Church comes to us in the eleventh chapter of *1 Corinthians*. In that chapter, Paul is writing with the simple purpose of correcting certain abuses which had crept into the local celebration ; and he presupposes, in his readers' minds, a knowledge of many details which are not matters of knowledge to us. But though his account leaves many uncertainties unresolved, yet he says enough to provide us with a fairly clear outline of the general plan and movement of the celebration, as it was observed in Corinth at the time of writing. Now that time was, roughly, twenty-five years after the death of Jesus. Had the Lord's Supper been celebrated in this same fashion throughout that quarter-century ? This is a fundamental question. The traditional belief has been that the Supper was celebrated from the very first in this, and in no other fashion. But during the last century it has become increasingly clear that very grave difficulties attach to this traditional view. For one

[1] For method of treatment, see Chapter I., p. 7 f. To obviate needless confusion in what, in itself, is a sufficiently confusing and intricate subject, it will be well to indicate here how the terms *Lord's Supper*, *Eucharist*, and *Agapé* are employed. In the course of this inquiry, we will use the terms *Lord's Supper*—or simply " The Supper "—and *Eucharist* indiscriminately, to designate the complete Christian celebration in any or all its forms and stages. The term *Agapé* will be omitted altogether, till near the end of our inquiry. In a short study like this, its earlier introduction would cause far more of confusion than of enlightenment. With the thing itself we shall be dealing all through our inquiry ; but it will conduce to clearness if, in the earlier stages, we put all thought of the *Agapé* out of our minds. The reason for this will appear in due course.

thing, there is no clear evidence to support it. References
to the Supper as it was observed previous to the writing
of *1 Corinthians* are not numerous, and they, all of them,
speak only about a " Breaking of bread." What was this
Breaking of bread ? The traditional view has been that
" Breaking of bread " was just another name for the
celebration described by Paul. No doubt this was a very
natural supposition ; but none the less it is nothing more
than a supposition, for there is no evidence to support it.
Accordingly it has come to be recognised by scholars that
any study of the Lord's Supper must begin from these
references to the Breaking of bread. What does the New
Testament mean when it says that the disciples met
together " to break bread " ? Our present chapter will
be wholly occupied with the endeavour to answer this
fundamental question. The following chapters will deal
with the Lord's Supper as described by Paul, and with its
subsequent development.

THE LORD'S SUPPER AS THE BREAKING OF BREAD

> " They devoted themselves to the instruction given
> by the apostles and to fellowship, breaking bread and
> praying together." [1]

> " Day by day they resorted with one accord to the
> temple, and broke bread together in their own homes." [2]

Luke, the writer of these words, was evidently impressed
with what had been told him of the attractiveness and
joyfulness of these repasts, for he adds, " they ate with a
glad and simple heart, praising God and looked on with
favour by all the people."

His language suggests, further, that the repasts were
real, hunger-satisfying meals ; and this is confirmed by
other evidence, notably Paul's account of the Supper at
Corinth, and the Supper-formulary preserved in the
Didachê.[3] It may be taken as practically certain that it

---

[1] Acts ii. 42.   [2] ii. 46.

[3] This *Didachê* formulary is given a few pages farther on.

was the evening meal that was thus signalised and made
the centre of the Christian fellowship. When the day's
work was done, they gathered to take their *supper* together.

These meals are here described by the verb, " they
broke bread " ; sometimes they were described by the
noun, " the breaking of bread." Now these terms are
never found, either in Greek or Hebrew, as designating
the simple taking of food ; always they imply that the
taking of food was accompanied, or rather, preceded, by a
certain formal and conspicuous action, namely, the pro-
nouncing of a blessing over the bread that was to be eaten,
followed by the breaking of the loaf in two, preparatory to
its distribution round the table. This was an old Jewish
custom, corresponding in part to our grace before meals,
but conveying far deeper suggestions of religious fellowship, and carried through with greater solemnity and
ceremony, and *reserved for certain meals of a more pronouncedly religious character.* The blessing was said, and
the bread broken by the presiding host, or head of the
household. On the occasion of the feeding of the multi-
tudes, as narrated in the *Gospels*, the ceremony was
performed by Jesus himself.[1]

In none of the early accounts of these Supper meals is
there any reference to a cup of wine. Neither in the
passages already cited, nor in the other three [2] which
exhaust the New Testament references to the Breaking
of bread, is any mention made of wine. The natural sense
of all these passages is that no wine was necessarily drunk ;
there was only the breaking of bread ; or, at least, that
alone had significance.

Now, when we turn to the *Apocryphal Acts*, dating from
the second and third centuries, we find frequent descrip-
tions of a type of Lord's Supper which knew only of a
Breaking of bread, and had no wine-celebration. Although these *Apocryphal Acts* are notorious factories of

---

[1] Mark vi. 41, viii. 6 ; Matt. xiv. 19, xv. 36 ; Luke ix. 16.

[2] Acts xx. 11 (Troas), xxvii. 35 (on the ship) ; Luke xxiv. 30 and
35 (Emmaus).

legend, they may, on that very account be accepted as excellent witnesses to the *popular* thought and practice of their time. In the *Acts of John*, we find the description of a Sunday's Worship, comprising an exhortation and a prayer by the Apostle, followed by a celebration of the Eucharist. This latter is described as follows :

> " And he asked for bread and gave thanks thus : What praise, or what offering, or what thanksgiving shall we, breaking this bread, name save thee only, O Lord Jesu ? We glorify thy name that was said by the Father . . . (*here follows a considerable and remarkable prayer, wholly occupied with ascribing praise to Christ*).
>
> " And he brake the bread and gave unto all of us, praying over each of the brethren that he might be worthy of the grace of the Lord and of the most holy eucharist. And he partook also himself likewise, and said : Unto me also be there a part with you, and : Peace be with you, my beloved." [1]

Again, in the *Acts of Thomas*, we find the description of a Eucharist, following immediately, as was customary, on the Baptism of a man and his family.

> " And when they, Siphor and his wife and daughter, were baptized and clad, the Apostle set bread on the table and blessed it and said : Bread of life, the which who eat abide incorruptible : Bread that filleth the hungry souls with the blessing thereof : thou art he that vouchsafest to receive a gift, that thou mayest become unto us remission of sins, and that they who eat thee may become immortal : we invoke upon thee the name of the mother, of the unspeakable mystery of the hidden powers and authorities : we invoke upon thee the name of Jesus. And he said : Let the powers of blessing come, and be established in this bread, that all the souls that partake of it may be

[1] 106–110.

washed from their sins. And he brake and gave unto
Siphor and his wife and daughter." [1]

Now, we are not at present concerned with the strange
type of thought disclosed here, but only with the *form* of
the celebration ; and these quotations, which are only two
out of several [2] that could be made, place it beyond doubt
that in certain regions, well into the third century, the
Eucharist was frequently celebrated in one element only,
namely, bread.[3]   Probably it is a Eucharist of this type that
is portrayed in some of the earliest second-century paintings
in the Catacombs, where Jesus is seated at table with his
disciples, apparently on the occasion of the Last Supper, but
the food consists of loaves and fishes, and the baskets stand
at the side filled with bread.[4]   In any case we have indubit-
able evidence that there persisted, till into the third century,
a type of Eucharist which bore the strongest family re-
semblance, *in form*, to the simple breaking of bread by the
primitive Church in Jerusalem.   Presently, we shall come
upon another, and intermediate, link in this family chain.

We come now to a highly important point.   In no one
of these accounts, in *Acts* and *Luke*, of the Breaking of bread,
is there any suggestion whatever that it was the *death* of
Jesus that was in the forefront of thought and devotion.
When we read of how they " ate with a glad and simple
heart, praising God," we catch the impression of a prevailing atmosphere of joyful thanksgiving for the blessings
of salvation, rather than of definite recollection of their

---

[1] 133. The *Acts of John* are not later than middle second century ;
the *Acts of Thomas* are third century.—M. R. James, *The Apocryphal
New Testament*, from which the above translations are taken.

[2] *Ac. John*, 85; *Ac. Thomas*, 29, 37, 49 f. ; *Ac. Peter (Vercell.)*, 5;
Clem. Homil. 14.

[3] In these *Apoc. Acts* and elsewhere, we also find Eucharists with
water used instead of wine. Probably the usual motive for this was
reluctance to drink wine, especially in the early morning.   The
substitution of water was made easy by the feeling that the essential
thing in the Eucharist was the bread, what was drunk afterwards
being of secondary moment, e.g. *Ac. Thomas*, 120 ; *Ac. Peter*, 2.

[4] Hunkin, *The Earliest Christian Church*, p. 6 note.

Master in the dark hour of his death. Some, who hold
that the death must have been prominent in the Supper
thoughts from the first, explain the disciples' joy as a result
of their apocalyptic hopes. But it is doubtful if even these
fervid hopes would have had power to fill their hearts with
joy if at the same time they were envisaging, through
vivid symbolism, their recent memories of the blow and
shock of the death. For at this early stage of their faith,
we have reason to think that, while the resurrection had
kindled their hearts, the death had still remained a thing
dark and shadowed with mystery. There had not yet
been time to search the Scriptures and understand that
the death had been integral to God's plan, and was indeed
the crowning act of His redeeming love. So there is a real
psychological difficulty in conceiving these earliest disciples
as centring their thoughts on their Master's death the while
they " ate with a glad and simple heart, praising God." [1]
In any case, there is never any suggestion in the records
that their thoughts were specifically directed upon the
death when they were engaged with the Breaking of bread.

We now turn to a witness of great importance, namely,
the *Didachê*, or *Teaching of the Apostles*, a document
which issued from the closing decade of the first century
or the opening decade of the second.[2] The *Didachê* not
only gives the outline of a formulary for the celebration

---

[1] There is a kindred psychological difficulty in regard to the Corinthian Christians. Can we conceive of them as engaged in a repast
which concentrated their thoughts on the death of Jesus the while
they snatched their food, let their poorer neighbours go hungry, and
sometimes even " got drunk " themselves ? (1 Cor. xi. 21). It is
tempting to surmise that, in spite of Paul's previous teaching, the
death-memorial type of Supper had never established itself firmly at
Corinth, and that Judaisers from Palestine had introduced the Corinthians to the simpler Jerusalem-type of Supper, which, with its note
of glad fellowship and joy, had proved more attractive, though fraught
with easy perils for people so volatile as they. Is not one of Paul's
counts against them that they had been failing to *discern the Lord's
body* in the bread they ate ?

[2] See Appendix A.

of the Eucharist, but also provides us with the first examples of eucharistic prayers that we possess. And once again there is no reference at all to the death of Jesus. And this is the more significant here, where we have to do with an extended formulary, and not merely with brief notices of a Breaking of bread as in *Acts*. It will be well at this point to set down the complete teaching of the *Didachê* on the Eucharist.

" On the Lord's day of the Lord come together, break bread and hold Eucharist, after confessing your transgressions, that your offering may be pure.[1]

And concerning the Eucharist, hold Eucharist thus : First, concerning the Cup :

We give thanks to Thee, our Father, for the Holy Vine of David Thy child, which Thou didst make known to us through Jesus Thy child ; to Thee be glory for ever.

And concerning the broken Bread :

We give Thee thanks, our Father, for the life and knowledge which Thou didst make known to us through Jesus Thy child. To Thee be glory for ever. As this broken bread was scattered upon the mountains, but was brought together and became one, so let Thy Church be gathered together from the ends of the earth into Thy kingdom, for Thine is the glory and the power through Jesus Christ for ever.

But let none eat or drink of your Eucharist except those who have been baptized in the Lord's name. For concerning this also did the Lord say, ' Give not that which is holy to the dogs.'

But, after you are satisfied with food, thus give thanks :

We give thanks to Thee, O Holy Father, for Thy Holy Name which Thou didst make to

[1] Chap. 14. What follows comes from Chapters 9 and 10.

9

tabernacle in our hearts, and for the knowledge and faith and immortality which Thou didst make known to us through Jesus Thy child.   To Thee be glory for ever.   Thou, Lord Almighty, didst create all things for Thy Name's sake, and didst give food and drink to men for their enjoyment, that they might give thanks to Thee, but us hast Thou blessed with spiritual food and drink and eternal life through Thy child.   Above all we give thanks to Thee for that Thou art mighty. To Thee be glory for ever.   Remember, Lord, Thy Church, to deliver it from all evil and to make it perfect in Thy love, and gather it together in its holiness from the four winds to Thy kingdom which Thou hast prepared for it.   For Thine is the power and the glory for ever.

Leader : Let grace come and let this world pass away.

Worshippers : Hosannah to the God of David.

Leader : If any man be holy let him come ! if any man be not let him repent !   Maranatha.

Worshippers : Amen.

But suffer the prophets to hold Eucharist as they will."

The arrangement of the material in the *Didachê* as a whole leaves no room for reasonable doubt that the first-quoted sentence (from chapter 14) refers to the same occasion as the remainder,[1] and that " this occasion is a Christian form of the Jewish common meal." [2]   The prayers are such as would be suitable for a religious repast, and have several points of affinity with the synagogue ritual.[3]

Now, here again, we have a real, hunger-satisfying

---

[1] Lietzmann, *Messe und Herrenmahl*, p. 232.

[2] Brilioth, *op. cit.* p. 19.

[3] Oesterley, *Jewish Background*, p. 131.   Also, see Lietzmann, p. 237, for the arrangement of the closing sentences in the form of a dialogue.

meal [1] which began, it appears, with the celebration of
the Eucharist, and closed with a prayer of thanksgiving.
But what we specially note is that in the whole formulary,
from beginning to end, there is no reference to the death
of Jesus, nor to the broken body or the shed blood. *Nor
is there any suggestion that the ceremony had originated
in the Last Supper of Jesus and his disciples.* Clearly this
is a type of Eucharist radically different from Paul's.
Further, the Breaking of bread seems to have been the
central thing in it. Not only chapter 14 indicates this,
but also chapter 9, where the distinctively Christian
thanksgiving is offered in the prayer over the bread, and
not in the wine-prayer with its recondite Messianic or
Apocalyptic content. Everything points to the bread
and its breaking being the central point in the symbolism ;
and the probabilities are that we have here a type of the
primitive *Breaking of bread* celebration, but in process
of transition towards a fuller form. The wine-celebration
appears to have been added at the beginning but not yet
to have been thoroughly incorporated.

In following these traces of a *Breaking of bread* celebration through the early centuries,[2] we have confined our

---

[1] " After you are satisfied with food."

[2] Two famous Liturgies have been preserved from the early
centuries, the *Liturgy of Hippolytus*, emanating from Rome at the
beginning of the third century, and the *Liturgy of Serapion*, emanating from Egypt about the middle of the fourth century. Both of
these contain clear traces of the primitive celebration. *Hippolytus*
gives a formulary of the *Agapê* (by this time a distinct and quite
subordinate rite) which follows closely the lines of a *Breaking of
bread* celebration, and diverges, in vital points, from a Lord's
Supper of the Pauline type. From *Serapion* we get a formulary of the
Eucharist itself, which reveals traces of the same divergencies. In
the Supper of *1 Corinthians*, and of the great main stream of Church-
practice which flowed from it, the Words of Institution form the
core round which everything in the rite is gathered. But in *Serapion*,
these Words are introduced in an explanatory and secondary
fashion, such that the rite would not *essentially* suffer though they
were excised from it. This indicates that in the *Serapion Liturgy* the
Words are an accretion and that in the original type out of which it

attention mainly to its form and general character. But we would find our conclusions strengthened if we proceeded to examine the content of thought and the style of diction disclosed in the eucharistic prayers. We cannot enter on that task here, as it would involve extended quotations. Lietzmann, however, has traced the continuity of thought and diction, and summarises his conclusions thus : " The prayers we have quoted from the *Acts of John* [1] stand midway between the *Didachê* and *Serapion* ; that is to say, they point to a living liturgical tradition, reaching from that most ancient of the Liturgies down to the Egyptian forms of the fourth century." [2]

To sum up. *In the Breaking of bread in* Acts, *in the* Didachê, *and in the* Apocryphal Acts, *we have evidence of a type of Lord's Supper much simpler than Paul's ; a type in which there was only the one element of bread, or, if wine did appear, its significance was secondary ; and a type which was in no sense a commemoration specifically of the death of Jesus. We find this type surviving in the* Liturgy of Hippolytus *at the opening of the third century, in its description of the ritual of the* Agapê ; *and, finally, we find traces of it lingering even in the Egyptian* Liturgy of Bishop Serapion *in the middle of the fourth century.*

So far we have been mainly concerned to establish the continued existence, through several centuries, of the *Breaking of bread* celebration, and to distinguish it from the Pauline type of Supper. We have been occupied, to a large extent, in determining what this Breaking of bread celebration was *not*. Now we must attempt the more positive and more delicate and difficult task of determining what it was. The task is made difficult by the meagreness of our direct information regarding the earliest celebrations.

developed there were no Words of Institution and no commemoration of the death of Jesus. (See Lietzmann, *op. cit.*, chaps. xi. and xii.)

[1] 85, 109.   [2] Lietzmann, *op. cit.* p. 242.

We have already seen that this earliest type of Lord's Supper took the form of a meal, and of a meal that was only *semi*-sacred. It was sacred, in so far as it was a meal of religious fellowship, not only with one another, but, in some way, also with Christ. On the other hand, it was only semi-sacred, in so far as it was a real meal, one of an everyday, hunger-satisfying kind. But this distinction which we naturally draw between the sacred and the ordinary element in the meal would have been largely if not wholly unintelligible to the Jewish Christians who were the first to participate in it. For even the most ordinary meal was no ordinary thing to them. Food was sacred ; it came to their tables, not simply from the shop, but from God ; and they never seem to have lost the sense that when they touched food they were near to God. In their national religion there had been a long history of sacrificial meals, reaching far back into the past, and though our knowledge of these is dim, it helps us to understand the *aura* of sacredness investing their meals, and the attendant conceptions of table-fellowship with one another and with God. This does not mean that crude primitive ideas were still vital in their thoughts ; but the atmosphere was still there, investing their fellowship with deep spiritual meanings which are by no means easy for us to recapture. The Essenes, for example, about whom Josephus has told us much, were in the habit of going to table robed in white garments, as though they were entering a sacred temple ; and they had a priest to say grace for them, both before and after food.[1]

But though all Jewish meals were thus lifted above the level of the " profane," there were frequent meals at which the religious motive was intensified, and the ritual element more pronounced. The Passover meal is the best known of these more special meals ; but there were others, of which we have information especially from the *Talmud*. One of these, which has been the subject of much inquiry of late, was the so-called *Kiddush*, or meal of *Sanctification*.

[1] *Wars of the Jews*, ii. 8. 5.

While the Passover was an annual event, the Kiddush took place every week. Its purpose was to greet the coming of the holy Sabbath, and to *sanctify* it. At some time after the Exile, certainly before the time of Christ, this Kiddush custom was established among the Jews. In this early stage the celebration was held in the home.[1] A family, or it might be, a company of congenial friends came together for a social meal, at some hour on the Friday afternoon. The closing hour or two of the day were thus spent at table, the meal being drawn out in conversation and discussion on religious matters lying close to their interest. Then, at dusk, when the Sabbath was about to begin, the meal was interrupted, in order that the head of the household, or the presiding host, might perform the simple but solemn rite of *Sanctification*. A cup of wine was brought, and a blessing said on it, a blessing first for the gift of wine, and then a special blessing for the gift of the Sabbath. In the present-day Jewish rituals and practice, this Kiddush cup is followed immediately by a blessing over a loaf of bread : *Blessed art Thou, O Lord our God, Eternal King, who bringest forth bread from the earth* : whereupon the loaf is broken and distributed. We cannot determine the precise differences between the ritual in the time of Jesus and the ritual of to-day. But in any case, one thing seems to be clear, namely, that the Breaking of bread was not then part of the special Kiddush rite (which appears to have exhausted itself in the Kiddush cup), but *marked the commencement of the meal-proper*. A second cup was brought when the meal had drawn to an end, and over this cup a blessing was said, which confined itself to a blessing for food. This closed the proceedings.

[1] " Heine, the German poet, who knew the life of the Ghetto, tells in one of his lyrics of the bent Jewish pedlar who takes off his pack on the Sabbath Eve and becomes a prince in his home. He becomes, too, a priest ; for it is a special characteristic of their religion that the religious ceremonial is part of the family life in the home."—Professor Norman Bentwich, in *The Listener*, November 23, 1932.

The close similarity of this simple ritual to the ritual observed by Jesus and his disciples at their Last Supper must be at once apparent. The bread and its breaking, the meal, the cup " when they had supped," the religious converse as they sat at table—all these essential elements of form are the same in both.

Meantime, however, our attention is not directed upon that one outstanding Last Supper with its unique significances, but must remain on the level of the Jewish meals, such as the Passover and the Kiddush.[1] These were held, in our Lord's time, not in the synagogue as later, but in the home. Frequently, as already indicated, they were family gatherings. But there had grown up in connection with them a custom which seems strange to us, but which was thoroughly congenial to Jews. Often it happened that a band of like-minded friends—chabēr, comrade—would form themselves into a club, or guild, or fellowship, as we would call it ; and the purpose of these guilds—chaburoth—was the simple one of holding religious meals in company. They met in one or other of their own homes in order to observe, let us say, the weekly Kiddush in the fashion already described. This Chaburah-habit among the Jews is an interesting parallel to the guild-habit we found among the people of the Graeco-Roman cities, but with a characteristic difference. The Jewish purpose was entirely religious, and confined itself to the partaking of a sacred meal in company, the while they conversed upon the things of God.

[1] The trend of opinion is now in favour of the Last Supper having been a celebration of the Kiddush, and not of the Passover ; held on the Thursday (as in John's *Gospel*) ; and taking the form of a Passover-Kiddush, for the sanctification of the holy Feast. This question can be studied in Oesterley's *Jewish Background*, 156–194, or in Lietzmann, *op. cit.* 211 ff. The latter gives a condensed and pointed summary of the evidence in favour of the Kiddush. But a decision on this question is not vital to our present purpose ; since we know from the *Talmud* this important fact, that *at every Chaburah gathering the ritual of Breaking the bread was customary*. The *Breaking of bread* was a constant feature of all such repasts.—Lietzmann, *op. cit.* 206.

It is well-nigh certain that this habit of clubbing together for sacred meals was firmly established and widely prevalent in the time of our Lord and his disciples. We have several indications of this in the *Talmud* : for instance, we are told how even Hillel and Shammai, the great Rabbis at the time of our Lord's birth, would engage in grave and lengthy debate upon the niceties of ritual to be observed on such *Chaburah* occasions. Now we reach a vital point ; and although what follows cannot be said to be demonstrated, yet the probabilities are strongly in its favour. Jesus, with his band of constant disciples about him, was to all intents and purposes the Leader of just such a *Chaburah*. Whether they ever formally constituted themselves as such, we do not know. Most probably they did not ; the bond uniting them was too deeply inward to want reinforcement from any formal, outward tie. Yet they were loyal Jews, devoted to the practices of their people's Faith ; and though they had small regard for the hair-splitting casuistry of the Rabbis, they faithfully attended the synagogue, observed the Feasts, and adhered, in general, to the religious customs and practices of their time. Would it not have been strange, therefore, if, possessing as they did so many of the characteristics and habits of a *Chaburah*, they had yet omitted to observe the simple, impressive, and truly spiritual rite of Breaking bread, which was the accepted and honoured custom in fellowships such as theirs ? It is quite true that we are nowhere told explicitly that Jesus and his disciple-band were in the habit of celebrating religious meals together. Yet that does not prove that they did not do so. The mere fact that the practice was a natural growth of Jewish religious life, and was so widespread and familiar, would account fully for the absence of special mention of it. In any case, we have a few positive indications in the New Testament that the custom of Breaking bread was no unfamiliar one to the disciples *during Jesus' life on earth*. On the occasion of the feeding of the multitude, we read that Jesus " looked up to heaven, and blessed and brake the loaves, and gave them to his disciples to set before them." [1] Again, *Luke's* account of the evening meal at Emmaus is specially significant. " *And it came to pass as he sat at meat with them, he took bread, and blessed it, and brake, and gave to them. And their eyes were opened, and they knew him. . . . And*—afterwards—*they told what things were done in the way, and how he was known by them in the breaking of bread.*" [2] This means that they did not recognise him till the moment when he took up the bread, and blessed it, and brake it. It would seem that there was something individual and peculiar about his customary manner of breaking the bread—whether in his action when breaking the loaf, or in the blessing he spoke over it—and it was this familiar idiosyncrasy of speech or of action that now gave them the key to his identity ; they " *knew him in the breaking of bread.*" Surely these Gospel narratives demonstrate this much at least, that at the time when the Gospels were in process of formation, *there were clear recollections of Jesus having been observed in the act of Breaking bread, on occasions other than the Last Supper.*

What we find, then, is a background of frequent and familiar religious meals which began with the brief, simple rite of blessing and breaking a loaf of bread, the breaking of the loaf being, like our cutting of it, simply the natural and necessary act preparatory to its distribution and consumption. And it is against *this* background—and not against the background of the one, unique, Last Supper—that we should seek to estimate and interpret the *Breaking of bread* in the Primitive Church at Jerusalem. After their Master had died and had appeared to them again in His risen glory, it was a most natural thing for his followers to draw together into a close fellowship, meeting for their

[1] Mark vi. 41, cf. viii. 6. The other two Synoptists also record the blessing and breaking of bread on these occasions. Matt. xiv. 19, xv. 36 ; Luke ix. 16.

[2] xxiv. 30 and 35.

evening meal in each others' houses,[1] that they might share their common experience and joy. And when they sat down at table, they would instinctively feel that they were met for a glad, yet solemn, religious repast ; and, perhaps without stopping to consider the matter at all, they would dignify the occasion by observing the simple, familiar, opening rite of blessing and breaking the bread. And then, as they watched now one, now another, of their company performing the simple rite, even as He had been used to do when he was among them, the stab of memory would waken to full life everything within them that belonged to Him. What more natural, at such moments, than that they should feel that they were in living fellowship with Him again, and that they were, in very deed, renewing the happy fellowship of the past ? We must not suppose that what they felt was a mere reaching out of their minds, and affections, and spirits towards Him. There was more than that. In some way they felt that He was really present with them at their table. They never seem to have felt as though they had lost him ; we never find them mourning for him, as all others, before or since, have mourned for their dead. They believed wholly that He was living, and living with them here and now. " *Where two or three are gathered together in my name, there am I in the midst of them.*" [2] It may be, as some hold, that these words were not spoken by Jesus ; but unquestionably they voice the belief of his worshipping people. He was present with them. In what way they conceived His presence we do not know; but that they realised it is beyond any doubt.

Such, then, we conceive the earliest Lord's Supper to have been. A simple meal of fellowship—fellowship with one another, but, deepest of all, fellowship with Christ. There was no cup of wine, or if, in times of plenty, wine did appear on the table, it had no special significance. The bread, which was always there, had no reference to the death of Jesus. Nor was there any thought of the Supper

[1] Acts ii. 42, 46.　　　　[2] Matt. xviii. 20.

being a copy of the last momentous Supper on the night
before the death.   Rather was it the simple successor of
the more ordinary fellowship-meals they had shared with
him during his life among them.   That which dominated
their thoughts as they joined in the blessing and breaking
of the bread was not the broken body of Christ, but His
continued presence in their midst as they sat at His Table.
The Presence of Christ—not his Death—was the keynote
of the earliest Lord's Supper.[1]

[1] On the whole subject, see Oesterley, *Jewish Background*, vi. vii. ;
Lietzmann, *Messe und Herrenmahl*, especially xii. xiii. ; Brilioth,
Eucharistic Faith and Practice, i.

CHAPTER XI

THE SACRAMENTS

THE PAULINE TYPE OF LORD'S SUPPER

THE type of Lord's Supper described by Paul in the eleventh chapter of *1 Corinthians* was destined to become dominant throughout the Church, and to be the basis of the various forms of celebration which are in vogue to-day. The Breaking-of-bread Supper, on the other hand, had no extended history. North of the Mediterranean, the Pauline type carried the day decisively ; only in Egypt and Ethiopia—regions where Paul's writ did not at first run—does the other appear to have flourished for some two centuries ; and although we find traces of it still lingering in the Egyptian *Liturgy of Serapion* (about A.D. 350), it is already being subdued and assimilated to the more dominant type. We may say, in general, that this primitive celebration shared in the declining fortunes of the Jewish-Christian Church. We call the other the *Pauline* type, because Paul is the first New Testament writer to describe it—indeed he is the first to give us definite knowledge of its existence as a rite of the Church. But many prominent scholars are being led to the conclusion that Paul has an even stronger claim to have his name associated with it. For it would appear that, in addition to his being our earliest authority for the rite, he was himself largely responsible for its adoption by the Church. In the present chapter, an endeavour will be made to set forth the main lines of evidence for this view.

Since the Pauline Supper claims to be a simple *replica* of the Last Supper of Jesus and his disciples, it is necessary, before proceeding to examine it, to have some understanding of the relation of Paul's account of that Last Supper to the other New Testament accounts of it, given by *Matthew*, *Mark*, and *Luke*. This is, of course, a very complex question even for experts, nor have they yet been able to reach agreed conclusions regarding it. All that will be attempted here is a brief indication of the present trend of opinion as to the relation of these four accounts [1] of the Last Supper to each other.

Matthew's account is directly dependent on *Mark's*. The close similarity is apparent. *Matthew* must have had *Mark's* account before him as he wrote, and he reproduces it with only a few minor modifications of expression, which make no material difference in the meaning of the whole. For our present purpose we may therefore leave *Matthew* aside.

Luke's account is very difficult to estimate. The text from which our English version has been translated gives a Supper having two wine-celebrations, with a bread-celebration between them. Happily we have strong reason for thinking that this unparalleled and incomprehensible arrangement was never described by the pen that wrote *Luke*. Our surviving manuscripts disclose, at this point, a quite phenomenal variety of text. There are manuscripts, or groups of manuscripts, giving some half-dozen different readings markedly diverging from that with which we are familiar. For instance, in one of these, verse 19 closes with the words, *This is my body*, and the rest of that verse along with the whole of verse 20 is omitted altogether. In another, verses 17 and 18 are omitted, while verses 19 and 20 are retained. The weight of opinion to-day is in favour of the former of these as representing what *Luke* originally wrote. That is to say,

[1] Matt. xxvi. 26–29; Mark, xiv. 22–25; Luke xxii. 15–20; I Cor. xi. 23–26. It is of great help to have the four accounts written out, side by side, in parallel columns, as they may be found in such studies as Lietzmann's *Messe und Herrenmahl*, chap. xiii., or Hunkin's, in *The Evangelical Doctrine of Holy Communion*, chap. i.

Luke's Supper would contain a wine-celebration with a pronouncedly eschatological reference, followed by a bread-celebration ending with the words, *This is my body.* Now this is a form which differs considerably from *Mark's* and *Paul's,* and it is easy to understand some copyist, while engaged in transcribing *Luke's Gospel,* endeavouring to bring *Luke's* account of the Last Supper more into line with the standard accounts by the simple expedient of adding at the end of *Luke's* account the words of verses 19*b* and 20, *which he borrowed from Paul.* Lietzmann, who accepts this short text of *Luke,* has further shown that though it differs considerably from *Mark,* it belongs to the same tradition as his ; and he contends for *Mark,* that of the three Gospel accounts his is the original and only independent one. Regarding Lietzmann's findings Brilioth has said that his vindication of the reliability of *Mark's* account is a result of permanent value, and must be a starting-point of future investigation of the problem.[1]

We are left, therefore, with the two accounts of *Mark* and *Paul* as our two independent witnesses to the Last Supper.   That they are independent, as literary documents, is apparent from their wide divergence in language and detail ;   on the other hand, they are as apparently in agreement on the general course and movement of the Supper.   Their skeleton-framework of the celebration is identical : *He took bread ; blessed it ; brake it ; and said, This is my body.   And he took a cup ; and said, This is my blood of the covenant* (or, *the covenant in my blood*).   The inference is that both *Mark's* account and *Paul's* sprang from the same tradition ; *Mark* perhaps being content to reproduce it with greater fidelity than was to be expected from the more independent and creative mind of Paul.

We now examine Paul's account of the Last Supper. Of our standard translations, the Authorised Version is here as reliable as any.

" For I have received of the Lord that which also I

---

[1] *Eucharistic Faith and Practice* (1930), p. 7.

delivered unto you, that the Lord Jesus the same
night in which he was betrayed took bread ; and when
he had given thanks, he brake it, and said, Take, eat ;
this is my body, which is broken for you ; this do in
remembrance of me. After the same manner also
he took the cup, when he had supped, saying, This
cup is the new testament in my blood ; this do ye,
as oft as ye drink it, in remembrance of me. For as
often as ye eat this bread, and drink this cup, ye do
show the Lord's death till he come."

When Paul asserts that he had " *received from the Lord* "
what he was about to impart regarding the Supper, we
understand him as claiming to be independent of human
authority. He is writing in the same strain as when he
wrote to the Galatians about his credentials as an Apostle
of Christ : " No, brothers, I tell you that the gospel
that I preach is not a human affair ; no man put it into
my hands, no man taught me what it meant, I had it by a
revelation of Jesus Christ." [1] In a similar vein, he now
claims that his assured knowledge regarding the Supper
had come to him direct from the Risen Lord himself. We
do not feel at home with an assertion like this, seeing that
it carries us away into what, for most, is an unmapped
continent of the Spirit ; and we should feel more at ease
if Paul's words could be shown to bear some more ordinary
meaning. But we must reckon with the undoubted fact
that Paul was a man who claimed to be the recipient of
special revelations from his Lord ; [2] and more than once
we find him determining his course of action by intima-
tions of the divine Will which had reached him in modes
transcending the normal experience of believing men.[3]
It must be to an experience of this kind that he refers
here ; the natural meaning of his words is that his special
knowledge had come to him direct from his Risen Lord.

[1] Gal. i. 11 f.
[2] 2 Cor. xii. 2 ; 1 Cor. xv. 8 ; cf. 1 Cor. xiv. 6 ; Acts xxvii. 24.
[3] Gal. ii. 2 ; Acts xvi. 6, 9.

Surely he would have expressed himself differently if he had merely meant that he had got his knowledge in the usual way, out of the written and oral traditions of the Last Supper, which, of course, reached back ultimately to Jesus himself as he spoke and acted on that occasion. Or, if he *had* chosen this rather unusual way of expressing that thought, surely he would at least have written, " I received it from the Lord Jesus," and not, " I received it from the Lord." The plain meaning of these words, coming from this man of visions and revelations, is that he had received his knowledge direct from his Exalted Lord.

But Paul cannot mean that what he received from his Lord was the whole detailed description of the Last Supper as he sets it down here. That would be a travesty of Revelation as we have been taught to understand it by just such leaders of Christian thought as Paul himself. A revelation of that kind would have been a gratuitous and needless marvel. The Church was already in possession of the facts regarding the Last Supper, and Paul had access to these facts ; indeed, the similarity of his account to Mark's shows that the detail of his knowledge was drawn from that Church-tradition. Wherein then consisted the new knowledge which his revelation brought to him ? Surely in this—that it was the Exalted Lord's will that the Church should adopt the Last Supper as the model for her future celebration of her rite. In other words, the core of the revelation was contained in the words which Paul places in the mouth of Jesus himself, " *This do in remembrance of me.*" As we have seen, Paul is our one and only New Testament authority for these words. May not this uniqueness be due precisely to the fact that the words were first mediated through a unique revelation given to Paul himself ?

In what form the revelation came to him, we are not told. Did it come in the form of some dramatic vision of the Last Supper and of what was said and done there ? In that event, the vision would be compacted partly out of materials of knowledge that had lain previously in

Paul's own mind partly from the new element of knowledge regarding his Lord's will concerning the rite. In this case, there would be no difficulty in understanding how Paul was led to put the words, " This do in remembrance of me," into the mouth of Jesus at the Last Supper. Had he not himself heard them spoken there ? However, it would be vain, even if it were fitting, to speculate upon the precise nature of Paul's revelation. But though we may never exactly know how he was led to include the words, " This do," in his record of the Last Supper, there are some considerations that might be helpful. It may quite well have been that Paul had never made any *exact* inquiry into what was said, and what was not said, at the Last Supper. For his mind was not of the type which finds an interest in determining the precise words that a speaker may have used, or the precise occasion on which he used them. We have an index of this in the fact that he never reveals in his Epistles any marked interest in the words of Jesus as spoken during the course of his earthly teaching. Paul must frequently have heard these great words quoted, and must have read many of them ; yet he practically never quotes them himself, nor even refers to them. His whole interest seems to have lain in getting behind the actual words into living contact with the mind of him who spoke them. Upon the *letter* of his Master's teaching he directed but little careful thought, because he had succeeded in absorbing its *spirit*, and to Paul that seemed the one thing that mattered.[1] Further, we must never forget that our modern standards of historical accuracy are very different from the loose standards which governed the thinking of Paul's day. We need only recall the striking lack of the historic sense evinced by him in his interpretations of Old Testament Scripture ; and we have already [2] commented upon the naïveté with which he discards the plain meaning of the Scripture words about the muzzling of the ox, in favour of a fanciful interpretation of his own, which we can see

[1] Cf. *supra*, p. 54.   [2] *Supra*, p. 83.

10

to have been manifestly untrue to the thought and purpose of the original writer. In the light of these, and similar considerations, we may understand how Paul might be but little disturbed by scruples, such as our modernly trained minds instinctively feel, about his attributing to the Jesus of the Last Supper the words, "This do in remembrance of me." Even if his revelation lacked that dramatic vividness which might have caused him to hear these words as actually being spoken at the Last Supper, we could still conceive of his being led, in all sincerity and honesty of mind, to place in the mouth of the Jesus who met with his disciples on that solemn occasion those words which, in strictest fact, had been words of the Jesus known to himself, the Risen and Exalted Lord.

One result we have derived from this study of Paul's account of the Last Supper is that the words, "This do in remembrance of me," were not spoken by Jesus on that occasion, but that he confined himself to such words as are recorded by the writer of the Gospel of Mark, our only other independent authority on the matter. This result, if it be correct, at once removes difficulties which attend the traditional view. These difficulties are such as the following. If Jesus instituted this rite before he died, why do we never once hear of it being celebrated during the first twenty years of the Church? Why do we hear, instead, of another rite, the rite of Breaking of bread, which has been shown to have been a celebration different in form, and radically different in content from the Last Supper celebration? Is it conceivable that Jesus could explicitly have said of that celebration, "Do this in remembrance of me," without being obeyed, from the first, by his devoted followers? Further, if this type of celebration was firmly established from the first, how are we to account for the undoubted existence in the first-century Church of the rite which is described in the *Didachê*, and which is not a memorial of the death of Jesus? These are real difficulties; but they are all removed if we accept the conclusion that Jesus had no explicit intention at the Last Supper of instituting a rite of the Church.

But, does not this conclusion, while removing one set of difficulties, create another in its place ? Brilioth, for instance, is sensible of this. He feels that such a reconstruction of the history empties the Last Supper of much of its deepest significance. While commending Lietzmann's researches as having produced results of permanent value,[1] Brilioth proceeds to challenge his conclusion that it was not till Paul's time that the Church rite became attached to the Last Supper as its basis and model. His one ground of challenge is this : " It is hardly conceivable that the accounts of the Last Supper should have been preserved and written down, unless they were regarded as describing the origin and the pattern of the regular religious meal of the Christian Church." [2] But why should it be " hardly conceivable " that the Last Supper should be recorded, except as describing the institution of the Church rite ? Is it not conceivable, for instance, that Jesus was concerned, at the Last Supper, mainly with the immediate crisis which his death was to bring upon the faith of his disciples, and that his words and his actions at the Supper were dictated by a simple desire to root in their minds the assurance that his death, which might well seem to be the ruin of their hopes, would prove to be in reality the divinely appointed means to their fulfilment ? May he not have been endeavouring to implant in them a way of looking at his death, which, when the blow fell, did keep their faith from falling to pieces, and so made it possible for them to be led forward to their resurrection-experiences—experiences which, on no reasonable hypothesis, could have happened to faithless men ? If this was so, then his words and actions at the Last Supper meant nothing less than the saving of their souls, and, so far as we can see, the saving of the cause. Surely a sufficient reason for their being recorded. Does

[1] *Op. cit.* p. 7.　　　　　　　　　　[2] *Ibid.* p. 12.

not the Last Supper become an even greater and more
decisive event, when viewed in some such light as this,
than when it is viewed, primarily, as the institution of a
memorial rite for the after-Church ?

The conclusion that Jesus did not, at the Last Supper,
definitively institute a rite for the Church dispels another
difficulty which has been widely felt. Many of us, in
our contact with the mind of Jesus, have been led to the
conviction that he was no institutionalist, in the sense
of one who stresses institutions or ceremonies as being
essential things. We are convinced that, for him, the
essential things in religion were only two—*Revelation* and
Faith—the Divine disclosure and the human response ;
that beside Faith all other human energies, or institutions,
or observances, are secondary ; that even the Church and
the Sacraments are secondary, existing only to serve
Faith ; and that the claim, often put forward for these,
that they possess within themselves a " divine right,
derived, not from their utility, but from their institution
by Christ," [1] is a declension from his spiritual conception
of religion. For those who feel thus, the elimination
from the historical Last Supper of these deeply treasured
words, " This do in remembrance of me," though at first
it may bring a pang of loss, must in the end prove to be no
loss, but an abiding gain.

Although our view of the Lord's Supper in the early
Church marks a departure, historically, from the view our
fathers held, yet, spiritually, it does not vitally differ
from it. For, in our view, the subsequent adoption
of the Last Supper as the model of the rite was a development in no way contrary to the purpose of Jesus.
No one can fail to recognise that the Lord's Supper,
when it came to be celebrated as a memorial of the death
of Jesus, was a more powerful and a more moving rite
than it had been when celebrated as a simple meal of
fellowship with the Exalted Christ. More than that : it

[1] Morgan, *Nature and Right of Religion*, p. 260.

became a more essentially Christian rite, since it kept the
thought of the worshippers firmly anchored to the person
of the historical Jesus. In this latter respect, it was far
in advance of the older rite. The central motive of that
rite had been, not the remembrance of the Jesus of history,
but fellowship with the Exalted Messiah or Lord ; and
when the Church had expanded beyond the narrow circle
of those who could remember Jesus and had become
peopled with Gentiles who had never seen nor heard him,
then something more definite was needed than a rite of
fellowship with the Exalted Redeemer if the worshippers'
minds were to be kept engaged with the Jesus who had
lived and died.[1] And so, it was a decisive step forward
when the Church's Lord's Supper became a memorial of
the death of Jesus. Henceforth, the thoughts of her
worshippers would never be allowed to wander far from
the Man who had lived on earth, and had died on a cross
at a spot near Jerusalem. And such a development was
entirely in line with the mind and purpose of Jesus. For
it seems clear that he not only desired to be remembered,
but regarded such remembrance of himself as indispensable, since he looked upon himself as standing at the
very centre of his Gospel. So, although we find ourselves
constrained to believe that his command, " Do this in
remembrance of me," was not spoken to the Twelve at
the Last Supper-table ; though we must believe, rather,
that he left them entirely free to be guided by their Spirit-
quickened instincts in their subsequent worship of Him ;
yet we also believe that it was His Spirit that led them
eventually to adopt the rite of remembrance which was
centred upon his dying hours ; in short, we believe that
our fathers made no error when they accepted the
command, " Do this in remembrance of me," as coming to
them from their Lord.

So far, we have confined our attention to the familiar
passage from the eleventh chapter of *1 Corinthians*, and

[1] *Infra*, pp. 208–213.

have assumed that Paul's conception of the Supper is to be found in it. This, surely, is the right method. There are references to the Supper in the tenth chapter,[1] but these stand on a quite different level from the deliberate pronouncements of the eleventh chapter. In these latter, Paul is expressly dealing with the Lord's Supper, and with nothing else. He has learned of certain abuses in the local observance, and, with a quite marked impressiveness and deliberation, sets himself to correct them by describing what he considers the right method and spirit of observance. But in the tenth chapter, the Supper is introduced in a wholly incidental way. There the specific subject is not the Lord's Supper, but Idolatry ; and the Supper is introduced simply as one of several instances which illustrate the perils of contact with heathen religious practices. Some of the Christians at Corinth had apparently been accepting invitations [2] from heathen friends to join them in their sacrificial religious meals ; and since these meals were social occasions as much as religious ones, they had thought they might safely enjoy the social fellowship without risk of being affected by the religious atmosphere and ritual, in which they would in spirit have no part. Paul's argument seems to be that there was very real danger in all this. To sit down as a guest at the table of a heathen god could never remain an indifferent thing, since it inevitably brought the guest into contact with what we would call " numinous " objects associated with that particular god, and such contact involved, as its consequence, some sort of real contact with the god himself. " You Corinthians know that this is so," says Paul ; " When you sit at the table of your own Lord, and eat His bread and drink from His cup, you know how you are brought into a very definite relation with Him." [3]

[1] Especially 16–21.

[2] One such invitation is preserved in a second-century papyrus, recently discovered : " Chairemon invites you to sup at the table of the Lord Serapis, in the Serapeion, to-morrow, the 15th, at the 9th hour."—*The Oxyrhynchus Papyri*, 110 and 523.

[3] v. 16.

Something like this appears to have been Paul's line of thought ; but the passage is extraordinarily difficult—one of the most debated passages that Paul ever wrote—and no attempt will be made here to unravel its difficulties, or to reconcile its thought with the conceptions that stand out clear from chapter eleven. The task has never been satisfactorily accomplished, although the best minds have wrestled with it. Many scholars have concluded that somehow the two chapters have come from different strains of the Apostle's thinking ; and though this is a very unsatisfactory conclusion, we may probably have to rest content with it, unless new sources of knowledge are tapped. It is tempting, however, to throw out the surmise, that the two strains of thought we seem to find in these two chapters are in some way parallel to the two strains of conception we have already discovered in the two types of Lord's Supper. In chapter ten we find what seem very like echoes from the primitive type of Supper. The emphasis is not on the memorial aspect of the Supper, as in chapter eleven, but on the fellowship aspect : the meal is pre-eminently a meal of Fellowship, at once with one another [1] and with Christ. [2] Then we note, also, the phrase *cup of blessing*, which was the technical Jewish designation for the cup of wine over which a blessing was said at the *Chaburah* meals. May it not have been that, although Paul had from the first taught the Corinthians to hold the Supper in his fashion, yet their celebration had come to be modified by ideas and practices derived from the earlier type, through the agency of emissaries from the mother-church who, we know, were active in Corinth ? This supposition makes it easier to understand how it was that some of the Corinthians could behave so badly at their Lord's table. [3] Perhaps also it would provide an illustration of the larger hospitality that the primitive type of Supper extended to mystical conceptions that were active in the Hellenistic environment of the Gentile Church, traces of which we can hardly fail to detect behind

[1] v. 17.   [2] v. 16.   [3] See *supra*, p. 128 n.

the language of the tenth chapter.[1]   It would also confirm
our conclusions as to the salutariness of the step which
the Church took when she abandoned that more simple
and hospitable rite, in favour of one which kept her thought
more steadily focused upon the Jesus of history who had
lived and died on earth.   For the rest, it would appear
that Paul had no profound antagonism towards the
primitive Supper.   Though he preferred his own type, yet
we find him at Troas celebrating a Breaking-of-Bread-
Supper, very soon after he had written the eleventh
chapter of *1 Corinthians*.   Evidently he would not re-
pudiate that kind of Supper outright, unless when it was
abused to an intolerable degree.

In any event, the best index to Paul's fundamental
conception of the Supper is to be sought in the deliberate
pronouncements of the eleventh chapter of *1 Corinthians*.
It is partly through failure to recognise this that writers
like Heitmueller, Lake, and, in a less degree, J. Weiss, are
able to discover, not only in the tenth chapter but also in
the eleventh, traces of the invasion of Paul's thought by
Hellenistic Mystery ideas.   These may easily be read out
of the language of the former chapter, but they cannot be
naturally read out of the latter, unless they are first read
into it.   There is nothing here about the Supper as
the avenue by which believers enter into mystical union
with Christ, or as being the means by which this union is
sustained.   Nor is there anything about a " real presence "
of Christ in the bread and wine, of such a kind that believers,
partaking of them, would receive elements charged with
supernatural powers.   The only suggestion of such an
idea is the words : [2]

> " He who eats and drinks without a proper sense of
> the body, eats and drinks to his own condemnation.
> That is why many of you are ill and infirm and a
> number even dead."

[1] On the difficult question of the extent to which Paul's own mind
gave sanction to such ideas, see *infra*, pp. 190–194.

[2] 1 Cor. xi. 29 f.

These words might suggest that the sickness was a direct consequence of the unworthy eating and drinking. But the words do not stand alone. Paul at once proceeds to indicate that such sickness and death did not issue from the partaking of the elements as their efficient cause, but were a consequence of the divine chastening and judgment :

> " If we only judged our own lives truly we would not come under the Lord's judgment. As it is, we are chastened when we are judged by him, so that we may not be condemned along with the world." [1]

In clear and positive terms Paul teaches that the Supper is essentially a memorial of Christ's death for men :

> " This do in remembrance of me. For as often as ye eat this bread, and drink this cup, ye do show the Lord's death till he come."

We have already seen that the former of these sentences is most probably a specifically Pauline formulation of the Lord's will. The latter is certainly Pauline, since it contains Paul's own added comment. And these two eminently Pauline sentences present the Supper as being, above all else, a memorial of Christ's death, and a means of " showing it forth." Whether this last term is to be construed with reference to spoken words accompanying the celebration, and so *proclaiming* the death ; or with reference to the whole celebration being a setting forth of the death in dramatic symbolism ; in neither case is there evidence of anything mystical or *sacramental*, in the stricter sense of the word. A memorial of Christ's sacrificial death, and a means of setting it forth—that is what, primarily, the Lord's Supper signifies for Paul.

[1] 1 Cor. xi. 31 f.

CHAPTER XII

THE SACRAMENTS

THE LORD'S SUPPER (*continued*)

SUMMARY OF RESULTS

IT may be well to summarise, in more severely historical fashion, the conclusions we have reached regarding the eucharistic practice of the early Church.

The evidence points to the existence of two different types of Lord's Supper.

(1) The primitive Jerusalem type was a fellowship-meal which began with the simple and familiar Jewish rite of Breaking bread. It was a continuation of the disciples' table-fellowship with Jesus ; and it conveyed to the participants a sense that He was present with them.

(2) The Pauline type also took the form of a meal, which began with a ceremony of Breaking bread and ended with the partaking of a cup of wine. But it was more than a simple meal of table-fellowship with the Exalted Lord and with one another. It claimed to be a continuation and reproduction, not of the religious meals that Jesus had been in the habit of sharing with his disciples, but of the one, unique, Last Supper held on the eve of his death. The bread and the wine were much more than representative articles of diet ; they had become symbols of Christ's broken body and shed blood, as in the Last Supper. The idea of table-fellowship was still retained, but the emphasis now fell on the new aspect of the Supper as a memorial of the sacrificial death.

A priori, there are three possible relations between these two types.

(*a*) Concurrently with the Jerusalem type, there might have been, from the first, another type, perhaps with bread only, but with the added words, " *This is my body.*" If so, this would be the prototype of the later Pauline form.

But there is no evidence for this, unless we were to accept the short text of Luke as pointing in this direction. Apart from this highly doubtful index, the evidence points towards the conclusion that the Pauline type originated in the Gentile Church, while the other had had its origin, and was to have its later career in the Jewish-Christian Church, and in regions, like Egypt, where Paul's influence did not prevail. Besides, it is doubtful if the primitive Christians at Jerusalem were sufficiently matured in faith for a confident and joyous[1] celebration of the death of Jesus. Their early feelings about the death seem rather to have been feelings of perplexity. The death remained something of a dark mystery ; or, at the best, a defeat gloriously annulled by the Resurrection. It would seem that, at first, they believed, not because of the death, but in spite of it.[2]

(*b*) The Pauline type might have been a direct development from the Jerusalem type, achieved in the Gentile Church through purely liturgical processes, by way of assimilation to the conceptions of a Dying-and-rising-again-saviour-god which were current in the Oriental Mystery-faiths.

This is a theory which has been seriously put forward as a solution of our problems. It is known as the *hypothesis of ætiological cult-legends.* We do not here expound it in detail. It should suffice to accept Lietzmann's matured pronouncement, that there is a wide gulf between the two liturgical conceptions—*bread broken for use at a fellowship-meal,* and *the Broken Bread as representing the body of Christ broken in death.* And this gulf, he main-

[1] Acts ii. 46.
[2] J. Weiss, *Urchristentum,* pp. 75–85.

tains, is so wide that no striving of the historian's imagination working along the lines of liturgical development has as yet come near to bridging it, often as the attempt has been made.[1]

(c) We are left, therefore, with the third alternative, namely, that the words, " *This is my body*," constitute an element which has not come into being through any mere process of liturgical development, but is an independent and original factor *with a basis in history*. That is to say, the evidence we have gathered from sources other than the Gospels regarding the Lord's Supper of the early Church, *demands* an historical Last Supper, substantially as it is described in the Gospels.

On the other hand, the evidence points to this Last Supper as not having been expressly ordained by Jesus to be the basis and model of a rite to be observed by the Church after his death. It points to our Master having spoken and acted at the Last Supper, primarily, perhaps wholly, with a view to meet the immediate need of the disciples in the impending crisis of their faith, and not with the purpose of instituting a rite. That is to say, the words, " This do in remembrance of me," were not spoken by Jesus at the Last Supper. The account of Mark is to be regarded as giving a true description of what he said at that Supper ; and when it was *first* written down, its simple purpose was to recount what transpired on that moving and memorable occasion, and not to explain the origin of the rite of the Church. For the rest, we may believe that the Pauline type of Supper—which is the Supper celebrated by the Church to-day—has always, from its first origin, stood in the very centre of the stream of spiritual life that had its source in the Master himself ; and that the Church has not been in error in believing that it was her Risen Lord's will that she should " do this in remembrance of Him."

<hr>

[1] *Op. cit.* p. 253.

SUBSEQUENT DEVELOPMENT OF THE PAULINE SUPPER

We have already indicated the later history of the primitive Jerusalem Supper,[1] which had a comparatively brief and restricted career. It was with the other type of Supper that the future lay.

In the Pauline Supper, which claimed to be a *replica* of the Last Supper of Jesus, the order of observance was : (a) Bread, (b) Meal-proper, (c) Cup.[2] But in the observations he makes upon the Supper, Paul's mind is evidently already working towards a discrimination between the ritual ceremonies of the bread and wine, on the one hand, and the meal-proper on the other. He says, for instance, that if people wish a substantial meal, they should take it at home.[3] Again, he lays stress upon the special sacredness of the bread over which the blessing has been spoken, as representing the body of Christ.[4] It is all still somewhat vague and indefinite ; but his mind would seem to be already on the way towards a differentiation of the ritual parts of the Supper from the more " profane " part. In any case, this was what took place ; and it is not difficult to reconstruct the probable process by which this differentiation took visible shape. First, the cup would be transferred from the end of the meal to the beginning. This would give the order : (a) Bread, (b) Cup, (c) Meal-proper ; with a unified and compact ceremonial rite standing out by itself at the commencement of the meal. The next step would be, that only one prayer would be offered, instead of the two hitherto required for the separately-placed Bread and Cup. It would be after this unification of the prayers that the custom would arise of calling this prayer the *Eucharist*—" giving of thanks."[5]

---

[1] *Supra*, p. 140.

[2] I Cor. xi. 25. Note the position of the words, *when he had supped.*

[3] 22. [4] 29.

[5] The Greek verb and its noun (*eucharistia*) are common in the N.T. to designate *giving of thanks*, especially for food, material and

It was now only a matter of time and circumstance for the final and decisive stage to be reached, namely, the complete separation of the ceremonial rite from the meal-proper and the union of the rite with the Word-of-God Service. First, we may assume, the prayer would grow in substance and length, thus adding impressiveness to the rite and emphasis to its separateness. Then, there came the time when, especially in larger centres, the church buildings were inadequate for a celebration of the Supper-meal by their increased congregations. To meet this difficulty it would seem that the expedient of sectional meals was tried. At least, this appears to be the occasion for some of the admonitions of Ignatius against disunion and lack of deference to authority. Behind his words we become sensible of a situation of strain and friction and incipient confusion, such as mark a time of transition.[1] About the year A.D. 150 we reach solid ground. From Justin Martyr we learn that the separation of rite and meal was, in Rome at least, by that time complete. The Sunday Service he describes is one at which the eucharistic rite was celebrated, having been preceded by the Word-of-God Service ; and there is no mention of participation in a meal. In different localities this combined separation and fusion would take place at different periods of time ; in Bithynia, for instance, it seems from Pliny's account to have been an accomplished fact in the second decade of the century. Probably by the end of the second century, the Church everywhere had taken this decisive step, which fixed the framework of the Christian Church Service, and produced " the classical type of eucharistic liturgy." [2]

---

spiritual. This is the only N.T. use. In the second century it is used often to designate the whole Lord's Supper rite. Also, more particularly, it is used to designate the eucharistic Prayer ; or even the elements themselves. All these uses of the word are appropriate, as indicating that *giving of thanks* was a dominant motive throughout the celebration. For detail, see Brilioth, *op. cit.* p. 20.

[1] *Smy.* 8 ; *Mag.* 7 ; *1 Clem.* 40.

[2] See *supra*, p. 66 f. ; Brilioth, *op. cit.* p. 25.

THE *AGAPÊ*

The Agapê.—What became of the meal, after its separation from the eucharistic rite ? It continued to be held in the evening—the Eucharist being now celebrated generally in the morning—and was now commonly known as the *Agapê*, or "Love-Feast." As a rule, the developed eucharistic rite was discontinued at the meal, and in place of it there reappeared the old, simple custom of blessing and breaking the bread. We learn this from the *Liturgy of Hippolytus*, and a group of Liturgies dependent on it, which contain, in addition to the eucharistic ritual, rituals for the *Agapê* as it was observed about the year A.D. 200 at Rome ; and although these rituals differ in detail, they present one fairly constant factor, namely, the Breaking of bread after the primitive fashion of Jerusalem.[1] In some regions, of which Africa was one, the evening meal, though separated from the eucharistic celebration in the morning, seems to have retained its dignity as a real eucharistic Supper, and began with the full rite. However, the history of the *Agapê* as a celebration distinct from the Lord's Supper lies wholly outside our period and cannot be pursued here.

The word *Agapê* is not found in the New Testament in connection with the Lord's Supper till we reach the Book of *Jude* ; and that is the only sure mention of it in Scripture. It occurs again in some manuscripts in *2 Peter* ii. 13 ; but scholars incline to regard it there as a corruption of another word, though Lightfoot and Bigg support the reading, *Agapê*. Jude introduces the word in connection with some supra-spiritual sect who inclined to be superior to certain moral laws :

> "These men are stains on your Love-feasts ; they have no qualms about carousing in your midst ; they look after none but themselves." [2]

Jude's words offer a striking parallel to the abuses in the

[1] Lietzmann, *op. cit.* xii.   [2] v. 12.

Corinthian Supper. Ignatius is the first writer to use the term *Agapê* freely. In the first two of the passages cited (at the foot of this page),[1] the reference is clearly to the Eucharist. In the third passage Ignatius writes : " It is not lawful either to baptize or to hold an *Agapê* without the bishop." As Lightfoot points out, *Agapê* must here again designate the Eucharist, since Ignatius is apparently referring to the two most important functions in which the Bishop could take part, and it would have been incongruous, in such a connection, to link Baptism with any lesser rite than the Eucharist itself.[2] Lightfoot finds no indication in *Ignatius* that the *Agapê* and the Eucharist had yet become separated. It is evident, therefore, that Ignatius uses *Agapê* to designate the same celebration as Paul designated by the term *Lord's Supper*. Referring to the *Didachê* eucharistic service, which was nearly contemporaneous with Ignatius, Brilioth says : " That the occasion is a Christian form of the Jewish common meal, a single act which is at once Eucharist and Agapê, may now be regarded as certain." [3]

There is no evidence, either in the New Testament or in the literature immediately following it, to support the view that the *Agapê* and the Eucharist were in some fashion separate things from the first. All our evidence indicates that, if *Agapê* and *Eucharist* were terms employed at all during the first century in this connection, then they were employed simply as interchangeable designations for the whole celebration which Paul designated as the *Lord's Supper*. Much needless confusion has arisen from the assumption (for it is nothing more) that *Agapê* and Lord's Supper were somehow separate things from the first, as in fact they did become separate later on. Probably the simple reason underlying this assumption is the unreadiness of our Western minds to grasp the fact that a meal was a sacred thing to a Jew, and that the whole Lord's

---

[1] *Eph.* xx. ; *Rom.* vii. ; *Smy.* 8.
[2] *Apostolic Fathers*, II. II. 1, 312 f.
[3] *Op. cit.* p. 19.

Supper, with its ritual ceremonies and its meal-proper, was in the earliest days a compact unity, one single, sacred celebration. It is very natural for us to distinguish between the sacred, ritual part of the Supper, and the more " profane " meal-proper ; but it is wholly unhistorical to carry back this modern distinction and impose it upon the Lord's Supper, as it was celebrated up to, and even beyond, Paul's time.

We have no evidence that the designation *Agapê* was used before, or during, Paul's time ; but it may have been, since the word gave fitting expression to one prominent aspect of the Lord's Supper, namely, its warm spirit of brotherly affection and benevolence. Tertullian [1] suggests that this was the origin of the name : it connoted *love in action*. But if the word was at all freely used in New Testament times, and before the definite separation of the rite from the meal, it was used to designate the same thing as Paul designated by *The Lord's Supper*.

When the separation did take place and the meal was held by itself in the evening, it very naturally fell sole heir to the name which had derived its origin from the warm fellowships of the whole celebration. As already indicated, the history of the *Agapê* as a separate celebration lies beyond our period ; but it may be said, in general, that with the passing of the generations the *Agapê* tended to degenerate, till it became a kind of charity-supper. After a few centuries it vanished altogether.[2]

[1] *Apology*, 39.
[2] On whole subject, see Oesterley, *op. cit.* chap. viii. Lietzmann *op. cit.* chap. xii.

CHAPTER XIII

The Sacraments

The Eucharistic Prayer

IN the New Testament there is no example of a eucharistic prayer, nor any indication of the specific contents
of such a prayer. In all probability this silence on the
part of the records is no accident. We have found strong
reason for thinking that in the early Church, during
its period of Enthusiasm, Prayer remained free. We may
take it as certain that there were then no *forms of prayer*
prescribed by authority, human or divine ; and as most
improbable that the forces of custom and habit had as
yet begun to operate with any strength in the direction
of standardising or stereotyping prayers. As late as
the end of the century, the prophet was allowed to pray
" as he would," even when presiding at a celebration of
the Eucharist.[1] It would be vain, therefore, to search for
traces of some standard form of eucharistic prayer in use
before or during the time of Paul. Such a quest would,
almost certainly, be a quest for something that never
existed.

The earliest eucharistic prayer that has come down to
us (apart from the brief *Didachê* prayers, which we have
seen to be prayers for a Supper of that primitive type
which the great Church soon left behind her) is the prayer
in the *Liturgy of Hippolytus*. " That this document really
represents the use of the Roman Church in the early third
century, may be regarded as established by the independent
researches of Dom Conolly and E. Schwarz."[2] In all
probability this highly important Liturgy, which took
shape about the year A.D. 200, embodies a custom of
prayer which had been in use even earlier. In any event,

---

[1] *Didachê*, chap. x.   [2] Brilioth, *op. cit.* p. 20.

famous Liturgy found in the eighth Book of the *Apostolical Constitutions* (which was most probably compiled in Antioch about the year 375),[1] these typically Jewish thanksgivings bulk so large that they would occupy about three pages of this book ; though this, in its turn, is also unique. In the prayer of *Hippolytus*, this Jewish element is wholly absent.

This raises a question which is still under debate. To what extent did the eucharistic prayers of the New Testament Church make use of the familiar Jewish material from the synagogue worship ? In the primitive type of Lord's Supper which was modelled, as we have seen, upon the Jewish family repast, the thanksgivings were primarily for the bread and wine themselves as symbols of the daily food and nourishment which God gives to man ; then, from that plane, they rose to thanksgiving for spiritual food and nourishment granted through Christ. These prayers, as the examples in the *Didachê* indicate, were probably largely Jewish in content. But when the Supper became modelled upon the Last Supper and concentrated upon the death of Christ, it is almost certain that the prayers would become more and more filled with Christ and His work. But did they generally become, like the *Hippolytus* prayer, wholly devoted to Christ ? This is highly doubtful. Justin in his *Dialogue with Trypho* [2] says that Jesus instituted the Eucharist " that we might thank God for that He has created the world and all that therein is for man's sake, and that He has delivered us from the sin in which we were born, and that He has cast down dominions and powers through him who suffered according to His will." Evidently Justin, about half a century before Hippolytus, was acquainted with eucharistic prayers containing the familiar Jewish elements. Brilioth thinks it " probable that the forms of worship in the Pauline churches were much more Jewish than that of *Hippolytus*, so far as real forms can have existed in a time of prophetic

[1] Linton, *op. cit.* p. 5.
[2] Chap. 41.

ecstasies and charismatic freedom." [1] Probably this is
true, although it may be an over-statement to say that
they were *much* more Jewish. There is one important
piece of evidence that should always be kept in mind. In
the designations of God which habitually flow from Paul's
pen, there is a striking absence of many of the designations
most frequent in the old Jewish prayers. Such epithets as
Holy, Strong, Great, Ruler-of-all, Mighty, King, Highest,
never appear in Paul, indicating the extent to which the
Jewish elements had become subordinate, in his prayer-
life at least.[2] On the other hand, these epithets become
frequent again in the second century, both in the literature
and prayers of Christianity. One thing is certain. In
the period of Enthusiasm, there cannot have been any of
that enlarging upon God's dealings in creation, providence,
and the history of Israel, which we find in some later
Liturgies. When the Enthusiasm waned and the conduct
of worship became the task of a few officials, familiar
Jewish habits of prayer would increasingly creep in. And
it was well for the Church that this was so. It was well
that her thanksgivings for Christ should thus come to be
set in a larger framework of history. " Had the cross
been commemorated as an isolated fact, it would have
been in danger of losing its moorings in history, and
drifting into the vague timelessness of a mystery-myth." [3]
But in the early days, when the Cross was still a recent
memory, this particular danger was not imminent ; the
fact of the death was then, by itself, a sufficient anchorage.
And generally speaking, we may feel certain that in the
Pauline churches of the first century it was Jesus—his
work, and death, and Risen Life—that provided the
dominant content of the eucharistic prayers.

(*b*) This eucharistic prayer of Hippolytus sets forth its
praises of Christ in a form which can be described as

Op. cit. p. 24.

[2] See the thirty-six Pauline designations of God, examined by
Von der Goltz, *Das Gebet*, p. 107 f.

[3] Brilioth, *Op. cit.* p. 280.

dramatic, or at least as *objective*. In commemorates
Christ's work in historical sequence. It passes in review
his coming forth from God, his incarnation, his fulfilment
of God's will on earth, his Last Supper, his suffering, his
death, and his Resurrection. Not once does the prayer
pass into the sphere of the human-subjective. Always the
adoring gaze is bent outwards, upon God and Christ, and
Their works and deeds of redeeming love.

Now, this objective poise of mind is constantly being
exhibited throughout the New Testament. It is exhibited,
with an especial magnificence, in the great hymn to Christ
as Lord which we find in the *Epistle to the Philippians*. In
that hymn the sweep of the thought is cosmic. Its magni-
tudes are God, Christ, and the World ; its theme, what
God has done for the World through Christ. Let the
hymn be carefully read over in this light,[1] and at once
we observe how neither the individual believer, nor even
the Church, appears on the colossal stage, unless it be
incidentally towards the end, among the vast multitude
of created beings who are seen bowing the knee to Him
who has been exalted to be Lord of all. Nowhere is there
the least suggestion of a subjective outlook ; from first
to last the gaze is held by the majestic drama of Redemption
as it unrolls itself out there, upon the vast cosmic stage.
But although this sustained objectivity of thought is
nowhere so arresting as in this great hymn, yet there is
hardly a page in the New Testament where we may not
be sensible of it as a prevailing habit of the early Christian
mind. Some day, perhaps, we shall understand this mind
better, when we have reached a surer knowledge of its
apocalyptic way of thinking. But there can be no doubt
as to the reality of this feature of it that we are now trying
to indicate. Always it is some objective work or deed of
God—whether it be acts of deliverance, or works of redem-
tion in the past, or whether it be some manifestation of
His living power in the present, wrought by the Spirit—
always it is something objective that is the final resting-

[1] See p. 119 above, where the hymn is quoted.

place for faith, or for contemplation.[1] We have already
found clear traces of a close kinship between these three
things in the early Church, *Thanksgiving-prayer*, *Hymns of
praise*, and *Credal-confessions*.[2] The key to this kinship is
to be found in this early habit of thought. The very
things which naturally go to the making of a creed were
just the things which, in his prayers and praises, the
Christian worshipper was expressing, or contemplating,
from day to day and from week to week. And here also
we find the key to that impression of massive weight and
strength which comes to us out of the greater prayers of
the Liturgies. They are monumental things, these
prayers ; built up out of solid masses of objective fact.
Sentence by sentence, phrase by phrase, they present to
us some fresh facet of the redeeming work of God and
Christ ; and in Worship, when the adoring gaze was led
from point to point of the soaring structure, the spirit of
thanksgiving awoke and poured itself out. And thus it
must have been from the earliest days.

(*c*) This eucharistic prayer of *Hippolytus* is entirely a
prayer of Praise and Thanks. Confession of sin is absent.
Petition is restricted to the request that God may send His
Holy Spirit upon the oblation of His Holy Church ; but
even this is to the end that " we may praise Thee and
glorify Thee." It is, in the fullest sense, a *eucharistic*
prayer. The thanksgiving motive is in complete ascendency
throughout.

These fervent thanksgivings were, primarily, the spontaneous outpourings of hearts deeply moved. They issued
from " the ache in the loving heart until it has uttered its
gratitude." [3] Intense joy and thankfulness express themselves as naturally and as inevitably in prayer as does the
sense of crying need. And although we will now pass on
to discuss at greater length some other aspects of this
Christian thanksgiving, we will not forget that this simple

---

[1] *Supra*, p. 45.
[2] *Supra*, pp. 117 ff.
[3] Welch, *The Religion of Israel under the Kingdom*, p. 128.

and obvious thing we have already said about it is perhaps the deepest thing we can ever say.

It has been already indicated that, in early Christian prayer in general, thanksgiving predominated over all other elements.[1] The truth is that thanksgiving stands on a quite different level from confession of sin, or petition. It is the prevailing mood of the Christian life. Thanksgiving, with Paul, for instance, is never just one among the exercises of faith, but is itself, psychologically speaking, the ultimate basis of faith, and also its final goal. Whenever God comes into a life with His goodness, thanksgiving is the inevitable response. To be a Christian is synonymous with giving thanks to the God and Father of Jesus Christ. " The more grace abounds, the more thanksgiving will rise and redound to the glory of God." [2] In this " rising and redounding of thanksgiving to the glory of God," there is something final ; for the moment, it presents itself to Paul as the highest result of grace. On another occasion, when writing to stimulate generous giving for the relief of the poor saints, Paul sums up with these words, " The service rendered by this fund does more than supply the wants of the saints ; it overflows with many a cry of thanks to God." [3] An even more precious result than the relief of suffering is the fresh flood of thanksgiving to God which it releases. Paul might quite well have described his own lifework as being just the task of awakening the spirit of thanksgiving to God throughout the whole world ; so closely was thanksgiving bound up with the essence of his religion.

Now, in all this, Paul was not expressing thoughts peculiar to himself, as is evident from the prevalence in New Testament times, and before them, of the conception of thanksgiving prayer as being the most perfect *sacrifice*, or *offering*, that man can make to God. The Old Testament already has the idea, as in Hosea's " calves of the lips," [4] or the Psalmist's " freewill offerings of my mouth." [5]

[1] *Supra*, p. 98. [2] 2 Cor. iv. 15. [3] ix. 11 f.
[4] xiv. 2. [5] cxix. 108.

We find the idea clearly expressed in *Hebrews* : [1] " And by him let us constantly offer praise to God as our sacrifice, that is the fruit of lips that celebrate his name." Justin Martyr [2] carries on the tradition of thought : " Also I say that the prayers and thanksgivings directed to God by the righteous are the only perfect sacrifices well-pleasing to God."

This brings us to an important question. During the time of the New Testament, was Worship—and the Lord's Supper in particular—associated with the idea of a sacrifice, or offering, made to God by the worshipping people ? And if so, wherein did the sacrifice, or offering, consist ?

There can be little question that there was this association. The New Testament itself exalts praise and thanksgiving, as we have just seen, to the level of a sacrifice. At the end of the century, the *Didachê* [3] speaks of the *sacrifice* that is offered in the Eucharist, though without further defining it. *Ignatius* and *1 Clement* [4] use Old Testament words, like *altar*, *oblation*, *priesthood*, evidently presupposing some correspondence between the Christian worship and the Jewish sacrificial system. Justin is more explicit, when he says, on the one hand, that Christ instituted the Eucharist that we might thank God for His gifts,[5] and on the other, that prayers and thanksgivings are the only perfect sacrifices. By the end of the second century, we find in the prayer of *Hippolytus* the idea of *oblation*, or offering, clearly expressed ; and from that time forward it appears in the eucharistic prayers of the Liturgies. So, although we have no very explicit New Testament evidence on the matter, we may feel certain that this idea of a sacrifice being offered to God in the Eucharist went back to the early Pauline Church at least.

But, if there was this idea of a sacrifice, it is equally certain that this sacrifice was no other than the simple and purely spiritual sacrifice that consisted in thanksgiving and praise. It was no sacrifice offered by a presiding

[1] xiii. 15.   [2] *Dial.* 117.   [3] 14.
[4] 40, 41.   [5] *Supra*, p. 165.

priest ; it was offered by the whole body of worshippers. It had no design of propitiating God, or changing His will ; rather, it was the simple, spontaneous, joyous, and solemn offering to God of the Spirit-quickened thanksgivings of the worshipping people. It is even possible that it was the *whole* celebration, and not only that part of it consisting of spoken prayers, that was looked upon as the *offering*. Augustine speaks of the whole celebration as the " visible word." Others have spoken of it, to the same purpose, as " an enacted prayer of immeasurable depth and intensity " ; " a dramatic act of commemoration and thanksgiving " for the redeeming work of God in Christ. There can be small doubt that the people of the New Testament regarded their Lord's Supper, and indeed their Worship in general, as conveying an offering to God—the offering of the people's thanksgiving and praise. On the other hand, there can be as little doubt that they went no further than this. Harnack has stated that until Cyprian's time there is no clear expression of the idea of a sacrifice other than that of praise and prayer ; and we have Brilioth's authority for saying that this statement of Harnack's seems to be generally accepted, even by Roman Catholic writers like Renz and Wieland, at least as regards the period before Irenæus.[1]

It is well to emphasise this conception of our Lord's Supper as containing an offering to God ; as being a *sacrifice of thanks and praise*. It is a mistake, surely, to reduce the celebration to a simple memorial of Christ's death, the virtue of which resides in the profound impression it makes on the mind and spirit of a true worshipper. Many will believe that its fundamental virtue lies in this region ; but they need not therefore hold that its function ends there. Something more results than the evocation of a series of subjective experiences. Something is actually *done*. An offering is made to God. " In worship, we do not only receive, but primarily we give. Worship is offering."[2] And our offering[3] consists in the

[1] *Op. cit.* p. 44.   [2] Simpson, *op. cit.* p. 23.   [3] *Supra*, p. 9 f.

thanksgiving of adoring hearts that have been stirred by a fresh perception of the wonder of God's grace in Christ. For thanksgiving is really our highest way of giving back to God of the grace that has come from Him.

Far more than in the contemplative East, our Western natures with their bent for the energetic and the practical need constant reminding that the offering which we should endeavour to make to God *at the supreme moment of Communion* is this offering of adoring gratitude and praise, and *not* the offering of *ourselves*, in the practical sense of rededication or renewal of our vows to Christ. After the Reformation, both the Church of England and the Church of Scotland introduced this idea of dedication and self-offering into their eucharistic prayers at a point *before* the act of Communion. " And here we offer and present unto Thee, O Lord, ourselves, our souls, and bodies, to be a reasonable, holy and lively sacrifice unto Thee." [1] But this has been changed, and our National Churches do well to-day in reverting to the tradition of all the ancient Liturgies and reserving this idea of self-offering until the prayer *after* the act of Communion, which surely is its appropriate place. The reasons for this are not far to seek. Some of the most desirable things—happiness for instance —are best secured by ceasing to strive for them and striving for something else instead—in the case of happiness, for such things as rectitude, love, trust. This deep principle was expressed for all time by the Master, when he said : " Seek ye first the kingdom of God, and his righteousness ; and all these things shall be added unto you." May it not be that *all these things* which we rightly seek as a result of Communion, and, chief among them, this dedication and offering of self, will most surely be attained precisely by this " method of indirection " ? In other words, we shall most surely attain to self-offering by ceasing consciously to strive for it, and by concentrating our attention elsewhere. As we sit at the Lord's table and *before* the act of Communion, it should be our effort to

[1] Church of England, *First Prayer-Book of Edward VI.* (1549).

forget, as far as may be, our own subjective selves, and to
keep our minds objectively poised, directed outwards upon
the works of God in Christ. The high forces operative
at the moment of true Communion do not reside with us ;
they reside with God. It is *Christ's Love* that *constrains*
us. Our part should accordingly be to suffer that divine
Love to exercise its full power upon us ; and we do this
most surely when we are content simply to contemplate
it, and to be moved by it to wonder and awe, to thanksgiving and praise. And then, when that Love has thus
taken hold of us, it will itself constrain us—to live, not
unto ourselves, but unto Him who died for us.

" The Communion Service should indeed be the
greatest of all Services. It should be encompassed
with dignity and with solemnity, and men should
take part in it only with penitence and the broken
heart with which the Lord is well pleased. But we
believe in the forgiveness of sin, and the Gospel is the
gladdest of revelations, and the Lord Jesus Christ
is the King of Glory. He is to be adored, He is to be
sung to, and we must learn to rejoice in Him. It was
a wise liturgical instinct which led the Fathers and
Teachers of our Scottish Communion Office to close
the great offering of its worship with this great
eucharistic hymn :

' O thou my soul, bless God the Lord ;
    And all that in me is
Be stirred up His Holy Name
    To magnify and bless.

Bless, O my soul, the Lord thy God,
    And not forgetful be
Of all His gracious benefits
    He hath bestow'd on thee.' " [1]

[1] Simpson, *op. cit.* p. 38.

CHAPTER XIV

THE SACRAMENTS

BAPTISM

IN strict order of treatment, Baptism should have come before the Lord's Supper. It has been reserved to the last for the following reasons. We know surprisingly little about the administration of the rite in New Testament times. Details as to its *where*, and *when*, and *how* have been left largely to surmise; only as to its *why* do we possess information solid enough to build upon. On this ground alone, it is difficult to incorporate the rite into our mental picture of the Worship as a whole. But there is a further, and deeper reason which adds to this difficulty. Baptism was a rite primarily for the individual believer, and not for the whole community of worshipping Christians. We cannot say to what extent the body of worshippers shared in the rite; we do not even know whether they were usually present in any numbers. Hence it comes that, in trying to visualise the early Worship, its rite of Baptism seems always to be hovering, dimly and vaguely, away in the background. The reader who is mainly concerned with the Worship as a whole might, without grave loss, omit this present chapter. On the other hand, we learn from the New Testament about the ideas which came to be embodied in the rite, and about its general significance for Christian thought; and it is well that we should explore this familiar track, especially since we can discover many links of communication between it and the main highway which the Worship of the community followed.

We will consider, first, the antecedents of the rite; then, its Christian significance; and finally, its alleged penetration by ideas of a strictly " sacramental," *ex opere operato* kind, issuing from the mystery religions of the Pagan world.

A. HISTORICAL ANTECEDENTS

In ancient literatures, worshippers are often enjoined to approach their gods with a clean heart, and a clean body, and even with clean clothing.

In the more primitive Faiths, certain people or objects were believed to be possessed with some noxious magic potency, or evil spirit, and they were regarded as *tabu*. Contact with them brought defilement, which required a lustral bath to wash it away. The water was supposed, somehow, to absorb the defilement, or to draw out the evil spirit.

In the Levitical Code of the Old Testament, a higher stage is reached. The notion of *tabu* is superseded by that of ceremonial defilement. The water is no longer regarded as having a magic efficacy, and the virtue of the rite rests solely upon its being commanded by God. In Jewish belief, no material thing could be, in itself, a vehicle of spiritual grace.[1] There is no evidence in Jewish literature that lustral washings were supposed, by themselves, to remove moral stains.

In Old Testament Prophecy, a still higher stage appears. For the greater prophets the rites have ceased to have vital importance, and the ritual vocabulary can now be used in prophetic exhortations, as supplying metaphors of moral cleansing.[2] It may have been this metaphorical or

---

[1] " The Jews regarded their sacred rites as divine commands, elements in a covenant of God of which they were the subjects. They were circumcised because it was so commanded, that they might remain within the covenant into which as Jews they were born. They offered sacrifices, because these were the divinely appointed means for maintaining and renewing their good relations with Jehovah. But they did not regard their rites as instruments of spiritual grace."—Gore, *The Holy Spirit and the Church*, p. 92.

[2] Isa. i. 16 ; Ps. li. 7.

symbolical language of the *Prophets* that suggested to John the Baptist the adoption of an actual rite, with a moral significance attached to it. His Baptism was a baptism of " repentance unto the remission of sins." This moral significance seems to have been set in a framework of eschatological thought. His Baptism appears to have been also a symbol of adherence to the company of those who " waited for the Kingdom of God."

It may be accepted as certain that the Christian rite was not instituted by Jesus. The command to baptize appears only in *Matthew*,[1] and with its Trinitarian formula it seems a later ecclesiastical addition. In the *Gospel of John*,[2] we are told that Jesus did not baptize, but that his disciples did. The writer must here mean the rite as practised by the Baptist ; for he clearly distinguishes Christian Baptism as ministering the gift of the Spirit, and that was a post-resurrection experience.

The closest analogy to Christian Baptism among the Jewish rites was the practice of baptizing proselytes. But the Christian rite cannot have been based on this. For the Jewish rite was designed for Gentiles only, to cleanse them from the defilements of their contact with Pagan gods and practices ; and it is inconceivable that Jews, who formed the bulk of the early converts to Christianity, would have submitted to a rite which equated them to Gentiles.

No one knows how Baptism came to be adopted by the Church ; but the most probable explanation is that it was under the immediate influence and example of the Baptist. The accounts given of Apollos,[3] and of certain " disciples " whom Paul found at Ephesus,[4] are highly suggestive. There is no solid ground for regarding these disciples, any more than Apollos, as disciples merely of John. They were already " disciples," believing Christians ; yet they knew of no baptism except John's. This seems to point to a primitive condition of things, in which, in some Christian circles at least, John's Baptism had simply been retained

[1] xxviii. 19. [2] iv. 1 f.
[3] Acts xviii. 24–28. [4] xix. 1–5 : *infra*, p. 186.

as a Christian rite of initiation. Its inadequacy would soon be felt, and there would be added to it the significantly Christian element of *calling upon the name of the Lord*.

At what time the full Christian rite came into being, we cannot confidently say ; but it must have been very early in the Church's career. Paul submitted himself to Baptism as a matter of course. Both he and the writer of *Acts* take it for granted as a universal practice. The New Testament invariably refers to it as if it had always been valid. Baptism forms part of the " elements of Christian doctrine." [1]

As to the form which the early rite took, we know little. Normally, it was administered to adults only. Occasionally, a whole household were baptized.[2] Usually, the method was by immersion in running water ; or in " other water," which might be warmed if required ; or by pouring water on the head. These, at least, are the directions of the *Didaché* [3] at the end of the first century.

A useful suggestion has recently been made.[4] It is shown that the Synoptic narratives of the Baptism and the Temptation of Jesus are written in the typical style of Jewish *Midrash*—the popular teaching of the synagogue, the " poetry of the Talmud," as one Jewish scholar calls it. *Vision* and *voice from heaven* are conventional Jewish methods of giving expression to things which are unseen (imperceptible to eye or ear)—it was in this fashion that Isaiah, Jeremiah, and Ezekiel had each narrated his call. Then a quotation is made from Origen, rebuking Celsus for his folly in treating the poetic symbolism of these Gospel narratives as though it professed to be a record of literal fact ; and regret is expressed that we have so few scholars like Origen, who refrained from translating Oriental poetry into bald, matter-of-fact, Western prose. After the Synoptic narratives of the Baptism of Jesus have in this way been vindicated as reliable records of actual *spiritual* experience, it is next shown that the teaching

[1] Heb. vi. 1. [2] Acts xvi. 33. [3] Chap. 7.
[4] B. W. Bacon, *The Story of Jesus*, chaps. iv. v.

12

of the original source from which *Matthew* and *Luke* drew
their common material was to the effect that Jesus regarded
his work as a continuation of John's and submitted himself
to John's Baptism, not as to a formal and half-meaningless
rite,[1] but as being the consecration of himself to the cause
of the Kingdom of God. If this was so, then Jesus
attached a deep significance to his Baptism, infusing into
it his spirit of self-dedication, even unto death if need be.
And if Baptism already meant this for Jesus, then, even
though he did not institute it as a rite for his followers, he
had prepared the way for their finding in it those larger
meanings which left John's Baptism far behind.

B. THE CHRISTIAN SIGNIFICANCE

John's Baptism had been a Baptism of "repentance
unto the remission of sins"; and this original and fundamental idea is carried over into the Christian rite. This
significance is explicitly attached to it by the writer of
Acts.[2] Baptism was the symbol of the break with the evil
past; the outward seal of an inner conversion, and of the
forgiveness of sins. Upon this foundation certain distinctively Christian interpretations were superimposed;
though we cannot now know the order in which this took
place.

(1) *Baptism implied a confession of faith in Christ, and
a dedication of the life to Him.*

Saul was baptized, "*calling upon the name of the Lord.*"[3]
Later, he wrote to the Romans,[4] "Whosoever shall call
upon the name of the Lord shall be saved." He describes
Baptism as *Baptism in*, or, *into the name of the Lord*. We
infer from these, and other indications, that at Baptism
the name of Jesus was invoked or pronounced by the
convert. Further, *James*[5] utters a warning against the

---

[1] As *Matthew's* addition of the words, *to fulfil all righteousness*,
seems to make it appear—iii. 15.

[2] ii. 38, xxii. 16.   [3] Acts xxii. 16.

[4] x. 13.   [5] ii. 7.

rich who " blaspheme the honourable name called over you." This suggests that the name of the Lord was *called upon*, not only by the convert, but also by the dispenser of the rite.

What is the significance of this *calling upon the name of the Lord ?* (*a*) Some hold that the explanation is to be sought from ancient mystical ideas about a person's name being part of his personality, in such a real way that knowledge of his name gave one power over him. Thus, one had only to pronounce the name of a god to have his power at one's disposal. Such conceptions, if strictly applied in the Christian case, would mean that the invocation of the name of Jesus acted as a kind of spell, bringing His power down to the worshipper, and placing it as his disposal. But surely we must demur to the suggestion that Paul, or Peter, or the early Christians in general, thought of the name of Jesus as acting in any such fashion. There is no evidence of this. The *calling upon the name* was not the only factor in the rite. Paul could speak of Baptism without introducing the *name* at all, as *Baptism into Christ*, or, *into his death*. In the later literature of the *Gospels* and *Acts*, we find references to exorcism in the name of Jesus, and these, in the opinion of some, are proofs of belief in a magic power attaching to the Name. But even if we were compelled by further evidence to assent to this view, nothing would be established beyond this, that magical ideas had invaded the circumference of Christian thought ; for certainly they had not, at that time, penetrated to its centre. The potencies on which New Testament religion staked its trust were never things such as spells and incantations, but things such as Faith and the Spirit. The whole trend of the literature demonstrates this abundantly.[1]

(*b*) Another ancient idea associated with the utterance of a god's name was that this act was a declaration of the god's right of property in the worshipper. The utterance

[1] The most distinguished exponent of these theories, (*a*) and (*b*), is Heitmueller, *Im Namen Jesu*, and *Taufe und Abendmahl bei Paulus*.

of the name stamped him as belonging to the god, in some such way as does the tattooing of a god's name on the body of his devotee. This idea of ownership may quite possibly have lain behind the *calling on the name of the Lord* ; at least, there is nothing in it to conflict with Christian thought. The idea would provide a very natural background for Paul's question, *Were ye baptized into the name of Paul ?*[1] That he belonged to Christ, as His bondslave, was a ruling idea with Paul.

(c) But it is probable that the primary idea behind the *calling upon the name of the Lord* was something simpler and more objective. There are indications that the earliest Confession of faith was comprised in the two Greek words, *Kyrios Jēsoûs*, which mean, *Jesus is Lord*. Thrice Paul repeats these words, and each time he leaves the impression that he is repeating a formula.

> " Every tongue shall confess that *Jesus Christ is Lord*." [2]
> " No one can say, *Jesus is Lord*, except in the Holy Spirit." [3]
> " Confess with your mouth that *Jesus is Lord*, believe in your heart that God raised him from the dead, and you will be saved. For with his heart man believes and is justified, with his mouth he confesses and is saved. . . . Every one who calls upon the name of the Lord will be saved." [4]

The sequence of ideas in the last passage suggests that Paul is referring to a confession of faith accompanying the act of Baptism. It is highly probable, therefore, that at Baptism the convert made open confession of his faith by repeating the formula, *Jesus is Lord*. This formula gave to Jesus his sovereign title, and when, through it, the convert " called upon the name of the Lord," he at once confessed his faith and gave himself in allegiance to his Lord.

[1] I Cor. i. 13.
[2] Phil. ii. 11.
[3] I Cor. xii. 3.
[4] Rom. x. 9 f. and 13.

(2) *In Baptism, the convert was received into the Christian community.*

There is only one passage where Paul clearly alludes to this aspect of the rite.[1] Paul's chief interest seems to have lain elsewhere, in the symbolism of the believer's union with Christ in the experience of death and resurrection. But it is probable that it was as the rite of entrance into the Church that Baptism figured most prominently in New Testament thought. Every religion of the day had its rite of entrance, or initiation. Judaism had circumcision for its own sons, and lustral washings for its heathen proselytes ; while John's Baptism had sealed those who like him were waiting for the Kingdom of God. But, quite apart from this prevailing impulse towards rites of initiation, the early Church was so compact a body, and possessed a consciousness of unity so deeply rooted and so sharply defined—both outwardly, in relation to " those outside," and inwardly, in relation to its Lord and Head—that it had within itself the strongest motive to adopt a rite of initiation, which would at once guard its door of entrance and serve as a seal of confirmation to those who were counted worthy to pass within.

An outstanding feature of this aspect of Baptism is the close connection that was believed to exist between Baptism and the gift of the Spirit, as shown in several New Testament references to the rite. Indeed, the association of Baptism with the Spirit is so close that it has led prominent scholars to maintain that the Spirit was *sacramentally* [2] mediated at Baptism. This aspect of the rite must therefore be carefully examined.

Two distinct stages of thought and practice, as regards

---

[1] 1 Cor. xii. 13.

[2] In this chapter the words *sacramental*, and *sacramentally*, are used in their strongest sense only, as implying that the rite was an actual vehicle of grace, *ex opere operato*. The words will be italicised, to indicate their specialised use.

the relation of Baptism to the gift of the Spirit, can be traced in the New Testament.

(*a*) In the earlier stage, the gift of the Spirit precedes Baptism. It was the belief of the early Church that possession of the Spirit was the one convincing proof of adoption into the Family of God. To be a Christian, one must be endowed with the Spirit.

> " This only would I know, received ye the Spirit by doing the works of the Law, or by believing the Gospel message ? " [1]
>
> " If any man have not the Spirit of Christ, he is none of his." [2]

In the earliest Church, the reception of the Spirit was a marked phenomenon, accompanied by striking manifestations in the recipient. The conversion of Cornelius is a case in point.

> " While Peter was still speaking, the Holy Spirit fell upon all who listened to what he said, and the Jewish believers were amazed that the gift of the Holy Spirit had actually been poured out on the Gentiles—for they heard them speak with tongues and magnify God. Whereupon Peter said, ' Can any one refuse water for the baptism of these people— people who have received the Holy Spirit just as we ourselves have ? ' And he ordered them to be baptized in the name of Jesus Christ." [3]

We may accept this account as containing a reliable tradition, not only because it bears marks of the early Enthusiasm, but also because it represents the gift of the Spirit as preceding Baptism, and this order of things was not the one most familiar and congenial to the writer of *Acts*. In the case of Cornelius, Baptism was granted only after unmistakable evidence of the gift of the Spirit.

That interesting person, the " private Christian," [4] of whom we have a glimpse in the Corinthian worship, throws

---

[1] Gal. iii. 2.   [2] Rom. viii. 9.   [3] x. 44–48.
[4] I Cor. xiv. 16 and 23 ; J. Weiss, *Commentary.*

light on this matter. He is a *private Christian*, not yet
baptized. He is a frequenter of the Christian gatherings,
special seats being set apart for him and his kind. He
takes part in the worship, to the extent of joining in the
Amen ; and is differentiated from full members of the
Church on the one hand and from unbelievers on the other.
He is evidently a kind of Christian proselyte, who has
given assent, more or less full, to the Faith, but has not
yet received baptism ; and the reason must be—here
we enter the region of hypothesis—that he has not yet
given clear signs of having received the Spirit. So he
waits, or is kept waiting, for the decisive moment when
the Spirit will descend upon him. When Paul writes
elsewhere, " God has sent forth the Spirit of His Son into
your hearts crying, *Abba ! Father !* " [1] he is probably
recalling a typical manifestation of the Spirit's working
at just such a decisive moment. The recognition of God
as *Father* is the distinguishing mark of the filial spirit ; and
although the *loud earnest cry*—as the Greek word for
" crying " implies it to have been—seems ascribed to the
Spirit within, it doubtless came to utterance on the lips
of the convert, where its very earnestness and its intensity
of joy and wonder evinced the Spirit's working. In such
ways did men of the first days show, by no uncertain signs,
that they had come home to God and been acknowledged
by Him. The gift of the Spirit was theirs ; and forthwith
they were baptized.

The New Testament conception, at least during the classic
period, appears to be that the gift of the Spirit is a
free and independent act of God. First, there is God's
call—also a sheer work of God ; [2] then there is its completion by the work of the Spirit ; and then follows
Baptism, as a more or less necessary completion, on the
human side, of what is already complete on the Divine
side. This subordination of Baptism, as a sort of visible
adjunct for human purposes to an already accomplished
and completed initiative of God, represents the thought

[1] Gal. iv. 6. [2] Burton, *I.C.C.* on Gal. i. 6.

of the Church in its early days and, we would maintain, the thought also of Paul.[1]

The reasons why Paul is believed to teach otherwise, and to present a *sacramental* mediation of the Spirit through Baptism, are largely drawn from two passages, which must be examined.

> " For by one Spirit we have all been baptized into one Body, Jews or Greeks, slaves or freemen ; we have all been immersed in one Spirit." [2]

There certainly is implied here a connection between Baptism and the gift of the Spirit ; but it is not asserted that the connection is one of cause and effect. The two things lay close together in thought, because they came close together in fact. In the early days, Baptism must usually have followed close upon conversion, as in the case of Cornelius. Besides, the rite itself must have been peculiarly impressive and moving, and must often have been the occasion for new and thrilling experiences for the convert. Hence it was very natural for Paul, or any one, to have the two things, Spirit-conversion and Baptism, running close together in his thought, and in retrospect, to look back to the latter, with its vivid and dramatic memories, as the landmark of the decisive moment.

> " Some of you, were once like that ; but you washed yourselves clean,[3] you were consecrated, you were justified in the name of our Lord Jesus Christ and in the Spirit of our God." [4]

Allowing that the reference in the *washed yourselves clean* is to Baptism, there is again a connection clearly posited between Baptism and the renewal of the life. Now, if we conceived Paul as writing with the precision of a careful theologian, we might have the right to insist that he must here be asserting that Baptism somehow initiated and

[1] Cf. Gunkel, *Die Wirkungen des Heiligen Geistes*, p. 28.
[2] I Cor. xii. 13.   [3] or, "had yourselves washed."   [4] I Cor. vi. 11.

governed the process of renewal, including the being
sanctified and justified. But, did Paul write, either here
or normally, as a precise theologian? Did he not write
rather as an eager missionary? And if so, was it not
more natural for his mind to fasten first upon the one
clearly visible and dramatic happening in the above
process of renewal, namely the baptismal rite, and then
to move *back* from that to the invisible workings of
God? Like other distinguished men whose function it
has been to reach and mould the mass-mind of their age,
Paul knew the value of a word-picture for getting his
message home.

We conclude that neither of these passages demonstrates the *sacramental* mediation of the Spirit through the
baptismal rite, since both can be quite naturally interpreted in a symbolical sense. In view of this, and of the
further fact that Paul frequently speaks of the gift of the
Spirit without reference to any visible rite, we shall require
much more solid evidence to convince us that a *sacramental* mediation is taught by him.

(*b*) In later New Testament times, Baptism came to be
administered in advance of any clear evidence of the
Spirit's working in the applicant, in the belief that the gift
of the Spirit would accompany, or follow, the administration
of the rite.

The *raison d'être* of this is not far to seek. There must
have been attached to every expanding church an increasing number of people who, though drawn to share
its fellowship, had as yet evinced no clear sign of Spirit-
experience. As time went on and the more striking
Spirit-manifestations grew rarer, the evidences of genuine
possession of the Spirit would become less easy to detect.
Thus there would emerge a pressing practical problem.
Ought the Church to continue to insist upon clear evidence
of the Spirit's presence, before granting Baptism? If she
did, she would keep a rapidly growing number of candidates
standing indefinitely at her door. We do not know the
stages by which this tension between Baptism and the

gift of the Spirit wrought itself out ; but we know the result. Baptism carried the day. The rite came to be administered where no clear signs of the Spirit had been visible. Candidates were probably now being carefully instructed in the Faith beforehand,[1] and in the end were baptized upon a clear profession of faith, in the belief that the gift of the Spirit would follow. Were they not now within the Church of God, which was the one earthly sphere of the Spirit's action ?

Of this change in practice we find evidence in the Book of *Acts* and elsewhere. Of the Samaritans [2] we read, that " as yet the Spirit had not fallen on any of them ; they had simply been baptized in the name of the Lord Jesus."

At Ephesus, Paul found some "disciples," whom he asked :

> " ' Did you receive the Holy Spirit when you believed ? ' ' No,' they said, ' we never even heard of its existence.' ' Then,' said he, ' what were you baptized in ? ' ' In John's baptism,' they replied. ' John,' said Paul, ' baptized with a baptism of repentance, telling the people to believe in him who was to come after him, that is, in Jesus.' When they heard this, they had themselves baptized in the name of the Lord Jesus, and after Paul laid his hands upon them, they spoke with tongues and prophesied. They numbered altogether about twelve men." [3]

Here a new element is introduced. It is not at Baptism, but afterwards at the *laying on of hands*, that the Spirit is given.[4] The evidence as a whole points to a time of transition, commencing probably about Paul's own time,

---

[1] As Heb. vi. 2 suggests.   [2] Acts viii. 16.   [3] Acts xix. 2–7.

[4] Other references to the laying on of hands are Acts viii. 17 (*after* Baptism) ; ix. 17 (*before* Baptism) ; 1 Tim. iv. 14 ; 2 Tim. i. 6. All precede the gift of the Spirit. Paul does not appear to have known anything of an established ceremony of laying on of hands as associated with the gift of the Spirit; and it is almost certain that the ceremony became established later, derived from O.T. practices. Cf. Deut. xxxiv. 9.

when emphasis came to be laid, first, upon Baptism, then, upon the laying on of hands, as precursors of the gift of the Spirit. Quite clearly, the door is now being opened for the invasion of *sacramental* ideas.

Our conclusion is, that Baptism was the visible ceremony, dramatic and impressive, which marked the moment of the convert's entrance into the Christian Church.[1] It marked the beginning of a closer relation with Christ. The Church was Christ's Body, and the convert now became a member of that Body, and was in permanent contact with Christ. All these things—the impressiveness of the rite itself, and its high significance as marking the entry upon a more exalted level of life in fellowship with Christ made it a memorable experience to the convert, and gave it prominence in the thought of the Church. That, in addition to this, it was a necessary and indispensable channel of grace, we cannot believe. Writing to the Corinthians, Paul appears to place a certain disparagement upon the rite, as compared with the preaching of the Word : " I am thankful now that I baptized none of you. . . . Christ did not send me to baptize, but to preach the gospel." [2]

(3) *Baptism became a symbol of the closest inner union with Christ.*

This aspect of the rite seems to have overshadowed every other in the mind of Paul.

" For all of you who had yourselves baptized into Christ have taken on the character of Christ." [3] (Perhaps Moffatt's translation of the final clause is too modernly conceived. It probably means : " you have become as Christ ; your standing is as his ; you are sons of God, as he is Son of God.") [4]

[1] It is possible that 1 Pet. i. 3–iv. 11 was originally an address given to newly baptized persons. So, Streeter, Bousset. Moffatt is adverse.

[2] 1 Cor. i. 16 f.   [3] Gal. iii. 27.   [4] Burton, *I.C.C.*, in loco.

" How can we live in sin any longer when we died
to sin ? Surely you know that all of us who have
been baptized into Christ Jesus have been baptized
into his death ! Our baptism into his death made
us share his burial so that as Christ was raised from
the dead by the glory of the Father, we too might live
and move in the new sphere of life." [1]

(The thought is further developed in the following
verses, and is taken up again in *Colossians* ii. 11 ff.)

It is evident that Paul's mind was greatly attracted
to this complex of ideas surrounding Baptism, as giving
wider expression to his deep sense of union with Christ.
He felt himself bound to Christ in a union more intimate
and mysterious than could be expressed in terms of the
personal relation of faith and love.   Many call it a
mystical union, and certainly it was one which baffled the
power of language to express.   Paul makes every endeavour
to express it.   Christ lives in him, and he in Christ : he
has been baptized into Christ : been crucified with Him :
been circumcised with His circumcision : has died with
Him : been buried with Him : been raised again with Him.

Now, we could understand these deep thoughts being
struck out originally by the strong and " mystical " mind
of Paul, but the trouble is that they do not all appear to
have originated there.   Paul implies that his Roman
readers were familiar with this *death* and *resurrection*
conception, and there is no reason to think that they
could have learned it from him.   Whence then did it
come ?   It is held by many that these ideas must have
passed into Christian thought from the Hellenistic
Mystery-religions, in several of which there was the conception, not only of a Dying-and-rising-again-saviour-god,
but also of a participation by the initiate in the god's
experience of death and resurrection, such that he became
one with his god.   It may have been that the general idea
of the believer's union with his Lord in the experience of

[1] Rom. vi. 2–4.

death and resurrection was suggested from this Hellenistic source ; but when it is asserted that the Church borrowed not only the general idea but also the Pagan implications behind it, then we must call a halt, so far at least as Paul is concerned. Some hold that it was Paul's belief that at Baptism a man became *divinised*, that is to say, had his nature changed in its very substance, so that he became one with his Lord in a sense never contemplated in the ethical and spiritual thought of Jesus. But it was against precisely this type of idea that Paul protested in the tenth chapter of *1 Corinthians*. Though the Israelites were baptized into Moses by the sea and by the cloud, and though they all ate the same supernatural food and drank the same supernatural drink, that did not safeguard them from so displeasing God afterwards by their evil deeds that most of them perished miserably in the wilderness. And that means, for the Corinthians, that neither the Lord's Supper nor Baptism could provide them with a sure and final salvation. If God's moral demands continued to be slighted or ignored, no washings, nor eatings, nor drinkings could avail. The only natural basis for such warnings is that the Corinthians must have been inclined to set an undue value upon the efficacy of mere rites. It was inevitable that some of them should do so, reared as they had been amid heathen fellowship-meals and rites of cleansing. The old man, plunging into the water, dies the death of Christ ; the new man, emerging as a Christian, undergoes the resurrection of Christ, and is thereby elevated above all further conflict—he is finally and absolutely saved. That is the inevitable logic of minds attuned to the conceptions of the Mystery-faiths of antiquity ; and in the third century of our Christian era it came to exercise a potent and distorting influence upon the general thought of the Church. But Paul combated this way of thinking, and combated it strenuously.

" It is difficult to resist the conclusion that Baptism is no more than a graphic symbol of what for Paul

is the vital thing, union with Christ in his death and
resurrection. . . . Whenever Paul touches on
efficient causes, he has recourse not to the rite, but
to the power of God, or to the working of faith, or
again to the working of the mystical union." [1]

C. THE ALLEGED INVASION BY PAGAN INFLUENCES

So far, we have been showing that the New Testament
language about Baptism can be construed in a symbolical
sense in accord with Jewish traditions of thought, at
least as naturally as in the thoroughgoing *sacramental*
sense of the Pagan tradition.   Yet, when all is said, the
fact remains that much of that New Testament language,
when taken in isolation, admits of being construed in terms
of Pagan thought.   It is necessary, therefore, to take a
step farther, and show that our symbolical interpretation
is not only a feasible one, but is actually more in harmony
with the general context of New Testament thinking.
For brevity's sake, attention will be confined to Paul.   In
the main, the modern theory, with its allegations of a
Pagan invasion into early Christian thought, stands or
falls with Paul.

When reading the literature of this modern theory,
with its extensive quotations from the Mystery writings,
its underlining of the parallelisms they disclose with the
thought of Paul, and its conclusions that it must have
been from this Pagan thought-world that Paul's conceptions were derived, one can hardly suppress the
suspicion that these writers have been carried away by
their theory into creating an entirely new personality, to
which they still attach the old name.   For their *Paul* is so
sympathetic to Mystery conceptions that we have difficulty
in recognising him.   Heitmueller attempts to explain by
speaking about Mystery conceptions being in the air Paul
breathed, like infective bacilli.   There is point in
Schweitzer's retort that bacilli are quite innocuous so long
as they are in the air ; they become harmful only when

[1] Morgan, *The Religion and Theology of Paul*, p. 211.

they have found a victim to offer a suitable *nidus*. Was
it likely that this Pharisee of the Pharisees would provide
a *nidus* for Mystery-bacilli ? Schweitzer's extreme suggestion, that the Apostle may quite well have absorbed
no more of Pagan thought than does a Roman Catholic
parish priest of the critical theology, is probably a closer
approximation to the truth than the view which makes him
a sympathetic Hellenist, with an abounding hospitality
for Pagan ideas.

It is very doubtful if the vogue of Mystery Religions in
the Græco-Roman world was as pronounced, in the first
century, as has been alleged. Such eminent scholars as
Wilamowitz and Edouard Meyer have insisted that we
have no sure proof of the efflorescence of Mystery earlier
than the second century after Christ. Waiving this point,
however, the most that can be proved is that, alongside
of Christianity, there were other Religions with general
conceptions resembling its own. But such parallelism
does not demonstrate identity of parentage, nor even
close family kinship. And when the new theory does
commit itself to bridging the gap between these parallel
manifestations, the results are far from convincing.

As a case in point, we take the Pauline conception of
the Spirit ; selecting it because of its prominence in
Christian Worship, and its close connection with Baptism.
Now, the modern theory does full justice to the place
which the Spirit occupied in Paul's religion. Indeed, it
does it more than justice, representing it as the one living
and decisive factor in his experience. It maintains that
every passage where Paul speaks of the Spirit, can be, and
ought to be, interpreted " in the light of Hellenistic speech-
usage." This is the method of approach gravely insisted
on by Reitzenstein.[1] And this might be a sound enough
method, if Paul had been merely a theological author who
published a new conception of the Spirit, based upon the
religious ideas of his time. But Paul did not come to know
the Spirit as a conception. It was the thing itself that

[1] *Hellenistischen Mysterienreligionen*, p. 163.

he knew. It had seized him, mastered him, taken possession of him. With his own eyes he had watched it seizing, and mastering, and taking possession of others. To Paul the Spirit was primarily a fact, an objective power that was invading the lives of men. And once these experiences of its power had come to him, there was no need nor inducement to look to Paganism for explanations of its meaning. There were ample clues to it lying to his hand in the ancient literature of his own people.

One crucial difficulty for the modern theory is presented by the *moral content* of Paul's idea of the Spirit.

> " The fruit of the Spirit is love, joy, peace, forbearance, kindness, goodness, faith, gentleness, self-control ; against such things there is no law." [1]

This is recognised to be one of Paul's most matured pronouncements on the Spirit. Now, could Paul have got *this* idea of the Spirit from the Mystery Religions ? Had they such an idea to offer ? No doubt, their initiates felt themselves uplifted, and even morally elevated, during their experience of becoming one with their god. But there is no evidence that it was a moral redemption that was sought. The things that were sought, and were believed to be secured, were things such as immortality, and union of nature with the god. Nor was this union, which was metaphysically and not morally conceived, capable of producing a moral renewal, even by way of by-product. For the personality of the god was in every case—Attis, Osiris, Serapis, Adonis, even Mithras—too vague, and mythical, and weak in moral content, to effect any such thing. So far, the modern theory has failed to make good its claims at this central and vital point.

But the Galatians passage carries us further in a positive direction, and illuminates Paul's idea of the Spirit and of its working.

We have Paul's own word for it,[2] that it was no light matter, when the gifts of the Spirit were being displayed

---

[1] Gal. v. 22 f.   [2] 1 Cor. xii. 2 f., xiv. 29.

in worship, to distinguish between an utterance that was
Spirit-inspired and one that was devil - inspired. At
Corinth, he is content to apply the test of *edification* : an
utterance which edified the community might be accepted
as inspired by the Spirit. And this was a good, rough-and-
ready, pragmatic test, adequate for the discouragement of
the more pronouncedly ecstatic and unbalanced manifestations, which was his main concern at the moment. But
obviously, this edification-test could not be final. *Edification* itself inevitably calls for definition. What precisely
are the specific things at which edification should aim?
Even if it were agreed that the final aim is moral edification, what exactly do we include under *moral*? The
question of the final standard is still unsolved. Now, it
is quite clear how Paul solved it. The fruits of the Spirit
which he enumerates as authentically genuine are obviously
just lineaments borrowed from his picture of Christ, and
more especially from those aspects of the picture—to him
the most moving of all—which present Him as giving
himself, in love, for men. " Love, joy, peace, forbearance,
kindness, goodness, faith, gentleness, self-control ; against
such things there is no law." In the last clause, what we
hear is the voice of the moral instinct. It is as though
Paul said, " I feel it in my very bones, that these are the
highest things in life ; they are final ; against such things
there can be no appeal." That is to say, the ultimate
decision is given by the instincts of the Christian conscience,
as enlightened by fellowship with the Exalted Christ, who,
for Paul, remained always clothed with the moral attributes of the Jesus of history. In Paul's innermost
religion there was a complex of closely associated conceptions of Christ. He was at once Spirit ; Indwelling
Christ ; Exalted Lord ; and Lord Jesus who had loved
him and given himself for him. But, whatever Paul
may have meant by " though we have known Christ after
the flesh, yet now henceforth know we him no more," there
can be no question about this, that neither his conception
of the Spirit, nor of the Indwelling Christ, nor of the Exalted

13

Lord, was ever allowed to pass beyond the control of the moral ideal presented by the Lord Jesus in his living and his dying.   At this point, we feel that we are in contact with the real, essential Paul—he was a man whose whole Christian life was in captivity of mind and will to the Lord Jesus who had loved him and given himself for him.   But, precisely at this vital point, we are far removed indeed from the thought-world which pervaded the Mystery Religions.[1]

[1] On the whole subject, see Karl Holl, *Gesammelte Aufsaetze zur Kirchengeschichte*, ii. Aufsatz 1.   Also, *infra*, p. 209 f.

CHAPTER XV

SUMMARY AND CONCLUSION

THE CENTRAL PLACE OF WORSHIP IN EARLY CHRISTIAN LIFE AND THOUGHT

WE have now completed our survey of the Worship of the Primitive Church, both in its general characteristics and its more detailed manifestations. It remains now to summarise our conclusions as to the outstanding place which Worship occupied in the life of that earliest Church. First, we will review our findings as to Worship being a central and dominant interest in the lives of worshipping Christians. Next, we will indicate more specifically the manner in which Worship shaped and controlled the course of Christian thought. Finally, we will sift out a few of its decisive influences on the Church's thought regarding her Master and Lord.

A. THE CENTRAL PLACE TAKEN BY WORSHIP

From all that we are told of the early Church and its Worship, it would appear that the immediate motive leading a number of Christians in any place to form themselves into a Christian fellowship was the desire to worship God together in their special Christian way. Their organisation as a visible body of believers was, first and foremost, an organisation for Worship. Organisation for other purposes might grow out of their Worship, or might lean on it, but was in no case primary. It was when regular assemblies for Worship were instituted in any place that the actual existence of a church in that place was attained, and its continuance secured.

We have reviewed the striking evidence for the central

place which the Worship took, through its Leaders of
worship, in the government of the Church—if so definite a
word as *government* may be applied to the guidance of
the Church's affairs through what were accepted as intima-
tions of the Spirit's Will.   The Leaders in the local worship,
the Prophets and Teachers, became, along with the
Apostles, Leaders in the Church's administration, in virtue
of their enjoying the most immediate access to the mind
of the Spirit ; and it was not until the worship-enthusiasm
waned that a different type of men—men of affairs, with
specialised gifts for rule and administration—gradually
gathered the reins of power into their hands.

We have also been able to divine something of the
central place which Worship held in *the life of the individual
Christian*.   Our historical survey showed that there is no
good reason to think that the activities of worship gravitated, to any appreciable extent, upon one day in the
week.   The slender evidences bearing on this question do
not conflict with daily, or at least frequent gatherings for
worship;   while the whole tone and temper of the early
Enthusiasm point definitely in that direction.   The impulses towards frequent worship were very strong.   It was
only in the worship-assemblies that the believer could
launch himself upon the broad current of the Spirit's
power ;   it was in fellowship with his Christian brothers
that he was able, most truly, to realise his fellowship with
Christ ;   it was upon church people that he must depend,
in the absence of written records, for his knowledge of
the life, and work, and example of his Master ;   and it was
from the warm intimacies and sympathies of the brotherhood that he derived the needed bracing for his difficult
life in the world.   We also found reason to believe that the
assemblies for Worship were the centres from which radiated
the streams of Christian beneficence.   The worship-
assemblies appear, in short, to have been the vital centres
which regulated the pulse-beats and controlled the whole
circulation of life within the early Christian communities.

Perhaps no New Testament writer realised the vital

significance of Worship for the individual so clearly as did the author of the *Epistle to the Hebrews*. He lived in the time of waning Enthusiasm, when defections from the Christian cause had become less rare ; and, as he observed the disastrous results in the lives of those who had fallen away, he had occasion, which earlier thinkers had happily lacked, to hold his Worship at arm's length, and consciously estimate how invaluable a thing it was. What we are referring to is not so much the fact that he conceived of religion as being essentially Worship—our knowledge of the background of his thinking is not yet sure enough to warrant our building conclusions upon it. But very clear, and very significant is the grave solemnity of those warnings and appeals which he throws out in the course of his writing, in an endeavour to persuade his readers to stand firm and remain staunch to their Christian fellowship. There is real passion in his description of the doom of those who fall away ; and it is evident, from the language he uses, that he looks upon their defection, not merely in the light of a disloyalty to the cause or even to Christ, but also as a falling away from the obligations and privileges which they have accepted in their worship-fellowship.

" For it is impossible for those who were once enlightened, and have tasted of the heavenly gift, and were made partakers of the Holy Ghost, and have tasted the good word of God, and the powers of the world to come, if they shall fall away, to renew them again unto repentance ; seeing they crucify to themselves the Son of God afresh, and put him to an open shame." [1]

The references here to Worship are apparent : to Baptism —*enlightened* ; to Scripture—*the good word of God* ; to the Spirit-manifestations—*the powers of the world to come.*

" Having therefore, brothers, boldness to enter into the holy place by the blood of Jesus, by the way which he inaugurated for us, a new and living

[1] Heb. vi. 4–6.

way, through the veil, that is to say, his flesh ; and having a great priest over the house of God ; let us draw near with a true heart in fulness of faith, having our hearts sprinkled from an evil conscience, and our body washed with pure water ; let us hold fast the confession of our hope that it waver not ; for he is faithful that promised ; and let us consider one another to provoke unto love and good works ; not forsaking the assembling of ourselves together, as the custom of some is, but exhorting one another ; and so much the more, as ye see the day drawing nigh. For if we sin wilfully after that we have received the knowledge of the truth, there remaineth no more a sacrifice for sins, but a certain fearful expectation of judgment, and a fierceness of fire which shall devour the adversaries." [1]

Again, he pictures for his readers the wonderful fellow-ship to which Worship gives entrance.

" Ye are come unto Mount Zion, and unto the city of the living God, the heavenly Jerusalem, and to innumerable hosts of angels, to the general assembly and church of the firstborn who are enrolled in heaven, and to God the Judge of all, and to the spirits of just men made perfect, and to Jesus the mediator of a new covenant, and to the blood of sprinkling that speaketh better than that of Abel." [2]

The man who wrote in the terms of these quotations had definitely realised that Community worship was the very breath of life to a believing Christian.

B. THE INFLUENCE OF WORSHIP ON THE COURSE OF EARLY CHRISTIAN THOUGHT

Modern research into the origins of Christianity has carried us far beyond the old idea that the Church started on her career equipped with the full panoply of Christian truth. We have learned to perceive that all that she

[1] Heb. x. 19–27.   [2] xii. 22–24.

possessed of distinctively Christian thought were a few burning convictions, based on immediate experience of God's redeeming work in Christ, and that there still lay in front of her the whole task of thinking out the significance of what she had experienced, of fitting that experience into the thought-forms she had inherited, and of discovering new forms which would express what had never been expressed before. Very astonishing are the rapidity and the sureness with which this task was overtaken. A wide distance separates the primitive conception of Jesus as Messiah, or apocalyptic Son of Man, from Paul's matured conception of the Exalted Lord who was at the same time the Indwelling Christ of each believer. Yet this wide distance was traversed in little more than a brief score of years. Nor was this accomplished by the labours of a few secluded thinkers. Such were not to be found in those compact fellowships where every man was labouring alongside of his brothers, and where even the greater men knew hardly more than did the ordinary disciple who had shared in their experience of the Risen Jesus.

" The truth is that nothing was formulated in the infant community. Such officials as they possessed were entirely untrained, thinking the same confused, tentative thoughts on the great subjects which had come to occupy their minds. Their teachers were the men who proved themselves most capable of uttering the common convictions and of impressing other minds. A situation of this type serves to stimulate and develop intelligence which a better regulated system often succeeds in sterilising." [1]

When we reviewed the Freedom which prevailed in the worship-assemblies, we found a condition of things which was highly stimulating to the intelligence, and enlisted all types of mind in the tasks of Christian thinking.

[1] A. C. Welch, *Visions of the End*, p. 173.

Amid the surge and ferment of thought in those Spirit-
quickened gatherings, new conceptions emerged and were
cast into shape.   Even as, in after years, the canon of the
Church's sacred Book was to be determined, not so much
by the decisions of a few superior intellects as by a con-
sensus of the general mind of the Church, so, in those
early days, the main lines which Christian thought was
to follow were laid down for it by the common mind of
the believers, as it declared itself in their worship-
assemblies.   There they sat, revolving in their minds
the great themes, till the moment came when the Spirit
impelled them to publish their thoughts in speech.   Any
one was allowed to speak, and all were encouraged to apply
their intelligence to sift out the truth in what they heard.
" Quench not the Spirit ; despise not prophesyings ;
prove all things ; hold fast that which is good." [1] Perhaps
a Teacher, or a Prophet, would give expression to some
fresh aspect of the manifold grace of God that had come
home to him.   If his new thought commended itself to
the experience of others, it would be caught up into their
minds, where it would fructify, and whence it would push
its way to utterance again, probably in some enriched and
developed form.   Thus it would pass from mind to mind,
being repeated, and developed, and repeated again, till
finally it became a part of the established currency of
the Church's thought.   By some such process of un-
conscious selection, new ideas were added to the permanent store.   And if this seem a haphazard way of
laying the foundations of a thought-structure which was
to command the reverence of the ages, let it be remembered
that the minds which thus tested the new ideas and passed
them into currency were minds which the Spirit of God
had stimulated to their fullest activity and sharpened to
their keenest insight.

And these minds that were thus laying the foundations
of Christian doctrine were minds that belonged to what we

[1] 1 Thess. v. 19 ff.

call *the common people*. Deissmann and others have rendered the great service of putting life into the dry bones of our knowledge that " not many wise, not many mighty, not many noble were called." [1] We can now visualise, in some fashion, those artisans, and merchants, and travellers by sea and land, those soldiers, and labouring men and women, and martyrs-to-be who were engaged in the Christian worship, and employed their everyday speech to give expression to the deep truths of the Gospel. This largely explains both the *sincerity* and the *universality* which marked their religious thinking. For these were men and women in touch with real life. They had not the temptation, which more leisured and cultured people often have, to regard religion as no more than an added interest and adornment to lives already richly stored. Their religion was, for most, the dominant factor in their existence ; for it was the power of God, giving them the mastery amid the urgent needs of their life. As a consequence, anything artificial, or fine-spun, or superficially emotional had small chance of survival in that atmosphere of reality and sincerity. Further, along with this quality of sincerity in their thinking, there was also the quality of universality. The joys and temptations of such people, their fears, and hopes, and sorrows, and sins were much as these things are the world over—outcrops of that deep-lying bed-rock of common humanity which is more or less the same in all. A divine message which could meet the needs of people like these was a message that would meet the needs of the whole world. And yet, if the formulation of that message had been left to some few secluded and sheltered thinkers among them, or had it been confined even to the greater Apostles themselves, with their less extended range of experience, it would have come short of that universal appeal which has been one of its pre-eminent characteristics. Universality was, of course, inherent in the Gospel of Jesus. Yet it might easily have been obscured, had it not been that the people

[1] I Cor. i. 26.

whose task it became to translate that message to the
world were people of a type that could penetrate to its
inmost essence, as a message for the deepest and most
universal need of man.

If Worship influenced thought through being the sphere
of an enthusiasm working upon minds of a certain type, it
influenced it also through being the sphere of a warm
brotherhood and love.   For love brings insight.

> " Every one that loveth is born of God, and knoweth
> God ; he that loveth not knoweth not God, for God is
> love." [1]

> " May you be so fixed and founded in love that you
> can grasp with all the saints what is the breadth,
> and length, and depth, and height, by knowing the
> love of Christ which surpasses all knowledge." [2]

These are merely two of the most familiar of many possible
quotations.   For the New Testament is very emphatic on
the matter.   Insight into the deep truth of God was not
the privilege of a few superior minds ; it became the
common possession of all who were instructed in love, and
who threw themselves into its mutual services in the
spirit of Christ.   Very significantly, it is into the very
centre of his discussion of Worship that Paul introduces
his glorious pæan on love.   Love, he asserts, is a more
potent force than hope ; it is more potent even than
faith ; it is the greatest of all the forces that reside in the
hearts of a worshipping community.   And among the
many other things that love can do, it gives insight into
truth.   Paul's wish for the Colossians, and for the
Laodiceans, and for others who, like them, had never seen

[1] 1 John iv. 7 f.

[2] Eph. iii. 17 f.   This passage, says Moffatt, " implies that brotherly
love is the condition of religious insight and grasp of spiritual truth ;
for whilst *love* is to be taken in its full scope, the special stress here
falls not on love to God, but on mutual love within the Church."—
Love in the New Testament, p. 174.

his face is that they may " learn the meaning of love " ;
that they may have " all the wealth of conviction that
comes from insight." [1]   And so the early worship-
assemblies, when they became the vital centres of a warm
beneficence and active spheres for the exercise of love, did,
by that very means, equip themselves for penetrating to
the heart of God's message of love, and also for expressing
it in classic forms which have been developed and enriched,
but have never been superseded by the subsequent thought
of the Church.

One of the most decisive services rendered by Worship
to Christian thought lay herein, that the mind of the
worshipper was kept steadily directed outwards, upon
Christ and upon concrete acts and deeds of God.
Probably it was because of this that, although the early
thinking was carried through by minds of the " common
people," yet it bears no stamp of the peculiar subjectivities
which often attach to minds of that type.   Keen and
urgent as were their own troubles, and needs, and wrongs,
their minds were never suffered to dwell broodingly, or
discontentedly, or resentfully, amongst these ; always they
were being pulled away to look outwards, in adoring
wonder, upon what God had done for them in Christ.   The
Incarnation, the obedience and suffering of Jesus, his
Death, his Resurrection—these, and other equally solid,
concrete, historical things were the steady objects of their
contemplation, and more especially when they gathered
at their Lord's Supper-table.   And if ever a subjective
bias of thought did assert itself unduly, it would speedily
be corrected by some fresh manifestation of the Spirit's
power, given within the actual place of worship—some
visible or audible display of that divine energy which had
broken anew into the world's life in Christ, and still was
manifesting its presence in their very midst.   This
objective character of their worship-thinking was clearly
exhibited, as we have seen, in their thanksgiving prayers

[1] Col. ii. 2.

and in their hymns to Christ and God, and became embodied, later, in their Creeds.

> " When the Catholic Christian kneels at the words *incarnatus est* (or at the words *and was incarnate*), he marks with proper solemnity his recognition that the Christian religion had its origin neither in general religious experience, nor in some particular esoteric mysticism, nor in a dogma, and he declares his faith to rest upon a particular event in history. Nor is the Catholic Christian peculiar in this concentration of faith. This is Christian Orthodoxy, both Catholic and Protestant." [1]

Those who would detach our religion from its historical basis and sublimate it into a system of idealism, or a religious philosophy, or anything of that kind, must not look for encouragement from the men who stood nearest to the origins of our Faith. There can be no question that in those hours when their religion became most vividly real to them, that is to say, when they were engaged in their united worship, their thoughts were objectively centred round certain specific happenings in history—round certain things which had been seen with the eye, and heard with the ear, and had become sensible even to the touch of human hands.[2]

C. THE INFLUENCE OF WORSHIP ON THOUGHT REGARDING CHRIST

One of our leading Christian thinkers has spoken of " the sovereign freedom with which the New Testament writers surveyed Christ, telling what they saw in books which have been justly described as literature, not dogma. Each looked at Jesus with his own eyes ; each spoke out of his own mind." [3] These words, we may feel certain, are applicable in substance to the Prophets and Teachers,

---

[1] Hoskyns and Davey, *Riddle of the New Testament*, p. 10.

[2] 1 John i. 1.

[3] H. R. Mackintosh, *The Person of Jesus Christ*, Introduction.

and to each contributor to the Worship-thought of the early Church. " Each looked at Jesus with his own eyes ; each spoke out of his own mind." We have no reason to think that the Church's thought about Jesus grew in any different fashion from her thought in general.

The closing chapter of a book is not the place to embark on an account of the movement of early thought regarding Jesus. The subject is a large one, and not a few of its problems remain unsolved. But there is one outstanding feature in that movement which calls for special attention, namely, the bestowal upon Jesus of the designation *Kyrios*, or *Lord*. It calls for attention not only because of its importance as marking a decisive advance in the Church's thought, but also because at this point the influence of Worship can readily be traced, or at least divined.

The conferring upon Jesus of the title *Lord* is recognised to have been " the greatest landmark in the history of early Christianity." [1] It marked definitely the transition from moral to religious veneration of Jesus. When the first Christians learned to say, " *Jesus is Lord*," it meant that they looked upon Him as an essentially divine being— one who stood upon the same level as God [2]—and that they paid homage to Him as such.

This marked a decisive advance beyond the days when Jesus was designated *Messiah*, or designated *Son of Man*. In the interest of brevity and clearness, we must leave the latter of these titles aside, as there are difficult problems still attaching to it. But with regard to the title of *Messiah* the general situation is clear. The Messiah was at best an angelic being, higher, no doubt, than others in that category, yet separated from God by the gulf which divides the creature from the Creator. Although the Messianic title proclaimed the profound impression which

---

[1] Morgan, *Nature and Right of Religion*, chap. vii.

[2] The equality with God was conceived at this early stage as one of *function*, not necessarily of *substance*—questions of *substance* did not emerge clearly into Christian thought until later. See Lohmeyer, *Kyrios Jesus*, p. 27.

Jesus had made on his disciples in his life, it fell definitely
short of placing him on an equality with God. It was the
designation *Lord* that marked their elevation of him to
that supreme level.[1]

That this decisive advance in Christian thought took
place at a very early stage, is no longer questioned. The
evidence of this is manifold, and reaches its apex in Paul's
Philippians' Hymn in praise of Jesus the Lord. The
Figure of the Lord is there conceived on a much vaster
scale than is even the Figure of the One like unto the Son of
Man in *Revelation*. He is Lord not only of the Church
and of his worshipping people, but of the whole created
Cosmos of God. He has been with God from the beginning, exercising the functions of God ; and when his
mission to the world is fulfilled, He is given by God the
name *Lord*, the name which is above every name because
it is the name of God Himself. The whole evidence for
the early bestowal upon Jesus of the designation *Lord*
has been summed up by a distinguished scholar in these
words: " That a few years after the crucifixion there was
in operation a fully developed cult in which Christ was
worshipped as God, no one now disputes." [2, 3]

We have now to estimate the part played by the Worship
in this decisive development. Clearly, a main motive
behind it must have been the Church's accumulating
experience of the *Power* of Jesus. Now, there were at
least two occasions in the habitual worship when the

[1] Lohmeyer, *op. cit.* p. 53.

[2] Morgan, *op. cit.* chap. vii.

[3] The publication in 1913 of Bousset's *Kyrios Christos*, stimulated
much controversy on the *Kyrios* title of Jesus. Bousset contended
that early Jewish Christianity never rose to the religious veneration
of Jesus as *Lord*, remaining content with a Son-of-Man Christology.
The worship of Jesus as *Lord*, he held, emerged in some Gentile
region, probably Antioch, where it was borrowed from the Hellenistic cults, in which *Lord* was the standing title of the saviour-god.
Critical opinion has now set definitely away from Bousset's thesis.
Lohmeyer's *Kyrios Jesus* is perhaps the weightiest answer that has
been given. Lohmeyer shows that Paul's *Kyrios* psalm in *Philippians* moves within the circle of Jewish and not of Greek ideas.

sense of his Power was quickened. Round their Supper-
table even in the earliest days, his followers were persuaded
that they still enjoyed his living Presence, and, we may
be certain, there came to them there, over and over again,
fresh experiences of his power over their lives. Further,
we must take account of the deep impression made by
the Spirit-phenomena in their midst. These were manifestations, primarily, of the power of God ; but they were
manifestations also of the power of Christ, for from the
earliest days the gifts of the Spirit were associated with
Him.[1] We may believe, therefore, that both of these
series of experiences—at their Lord's Supper, and in their
more ordinary worship—must have played no small part
in the process which issued in the triumphant designation
of Him as *Lord of all*. Yet most will feel that not all the
Spirit-phenomena in the world could have persuaded these
Jewish-bred Christians of the propriety of bestowing,
even upon their Messiah, the name which hitherto had
been jealously reserved for God Himself, unless they had
been convinced, *on other grounds*, that Jesus was worthy
so to be called. That is to say, we must look for the final
source of this high designation in the impression made on
them by the life and the person of Jesus when he was on
earth. It had been an impression of *Power*—of quite
unique power. It had been the impression, somehow, of
a sovereign personality. The roots of their final designation of him as Lord must have lain there. They struck
deeper into their faith when the death came, and when its
crushing sense of defeat was gloriously annulled by the
Resurrection ; deeper still, when they commenced to
gather for worship, and day after day revived their fellowship with Him and felt his power tightening on their lives ;
deeper still, when, at Pentecost and often afterwards, the
Spirit broke into their midst, endowing them anew with
gifts of his Power from on high. Then at last, it fell to
some one, we know not whom—some Apostle perhaps, or
perhaps some Prophet in a moment of rapt vision during

[1] *Supra*, p. 25 f.

worship—to crystallise into a single word these profound impressions that the Redeemer had made ; and so was brought to birth the greatest of all the Church's Confessions, " Jesus is *Lord*."

But the battle was far from won when this triumphant advance had been accomplished. A great territory had been conquered in the name of faith ; but if this conquest was to be a source of strength and not of weakness, the new gains had imperatively to be consolidated. And the need was pressing. The Church's mind was in its most plastic and formative period. If its faith, at this stage, had been suffered to lose firm hold of the Jesus who had lived and died, the results would have been disastrous for all after-time. And the risk that this might happen was very real. There was imminent danger that the thought of the Church might become unmoored from its anchorage in the Jesus of history, and drift away into vague and vagrant speculation about the Exalted Lord. Let us get hold of this.

In each of the great designations successively bestowed upon Jesus—such as *Messiah, Son of Man, Lord*—there are two distinct elements of thought-content which we should endeavour to hold apart in our thinking. The one of these is an element more or less mythological,[1] speculative, theoretical, and abstract, borrowed from the contemporary world of religious thought. The other is the personal element, derived from immediate knowledge or experience of Jesus himself—his Life, his Work, his Person, his Power. The latter of these elements is the vital and the continuous one ; the other is more of the nature of a convenient framework, being some contemporary thought-form, the noblest and loftiest available at the time, taken over by the Church to serve as a vehicle for carrying her accumulating experience of Jesus and her growing thought about Him, but destined to be superseded, or supplemented, once it proved itself inadequate, by some other thought-form, still loftier and more comprehensive. It was thus

[1] In the better sense of the word.

that the earlier designations, *Messiah* and *Son of Man*,
gave way to the later, and loftier designation, *Lord.*

Now, if continuity was to be secured for the growing
thought about Jesus, as it thus passed from one category
into another, one condition was necessary, namely, that
the personal element in each new designation should
become strong enough to subdue, to define, and in some
measure even to absorb the speculative and abstract
element. And when the new designation *Lord* was
adopted, there was real danger that this condition might be
lacking. Of course, there was no such danger in the case
of those who had known Jesus when he was on earth. In
their case, the personal element was primary and determinative in whatever designation they might give him.
For them, the identification of Jesus with the *Lord* was
equally an identification of the *Lord* with Jesus ; in other
words, their *Lord* was clothed from the first, and remained
clothed, with the personal attributes of Jesus. But in the
case of others who had never known the Jesus of earth,
the position was entirely different. Their primary knowledge was knowledge not so much of Jesus as of the Exalted
Messiah, or *Lord*. There was Paul, for instance, the
chief among that growing multitude whose devotion was
given, not initially to Jesus, but to the Risen and Glorified
Lord. From the day of Paul's conversion, his Redeemer
was clothed in the divine radiance and heavenly glory in
which He had first appeared to him. But Paul's thought
about his *Lord* did not for long remain directed thus
intently upwards ; it soon was taught to move back-
wards, towards the Jesus of history. We are not told
when he first learned his detail of the life and person of
Jesus ; certainly he must have learned much during that
fortnight he spent with Peter in the capital.[1] In any
case, the logic of Paul's own thinking about his *Lord* must
have quickened his desire for knowledge of Jesus and
stimulated his zest for inquiry about him. For Paul
could not think about his Lord without thinking about the

[1] Gal. i. 18.

14

cross He bore; nor could he think of the cross without
thinking, and wondering, about him who had died there.
In short, "we must conclude that his mind started from
the Risen One who encountered him in glory at Damascus,
moved thence to the cross, which the Lord had endured,
and came finally to rest on the person of the Crucified." [1]
In Paul's case, the desired result was thus attained; his
thought became firmly anchored to the Jesus who had
lived and died. *How was this result attained in the case of
those many who did not enjoy Paul's advantages—the advantages of a vivid revelation and of intimate contact with
men who had known Jesus?*

There was the *Diaspora* Jew, for instance, in some
remote outpost of the Church. When he became a
Christian, his primary allegiance was to the glorified
Messiah of his People. Of the Jesus who had lived and
had died at Calvary he probably knew little—perhaps
not more than the outline-story of his life and death.[2]
But his new-born faith needed more than that for its
nourishment. And what it needed was something which
his abstract *Messiah*-conception did not possess within
itself to give. For the *Messiah* was a vague, and undefined, and not very attractive Figure. " There is nothing
lovable about the Jewish Messiah. In Judaism the work
of the Messiah is an abrupt display of the power of God,
acting through one who, worthy of all honour, no doubt,
for what he does, is only an instrument, showing in his
life, apart from his success, no such attractiveness or
extraordinary personality as would lead men to risk
danger or death for his dear sake." [3] Clearly, no such
Jewish convert as we are picturing could ever have grown
to be a devoted servant of the Lord Jesus Christ, loyal
to Him in life and through death, on the strength of his

[1] Mackintosh, *The Person of Jesus Christ*, p. 53 ; cf. Deissmann,
St. Paul, especially chap. vii.

[2] J. Weiss, *Urchristentum*, p. 166.

[3] Lukyn Williams, *The Hebrew Christian Messiah*, p. 272 ; cf.
J. Weiss, *op. cit.* p. 25.

initial belief in the exalted *Messiah*. It was indispensable
that he should be brought into intimate touch with the
Jesus who had lived and died ; that his slender knowledge
of him should be filled in with illuminating and moving
detail ; that his *Messiah* should become instinct with
the personality of Jesus ; that his thought, in short, should
travel back, as Paul's thought did, to the Jesus who died
on the cross, and should find its resting-place upon the
clearly realised person of the Crucified. *In the case of this
Jewish convert, how was this result attained ?*

Then there was the Gentile convert. In his case the
problem would be apt to be even more acute. For when
the Gentile became a Christian, he probably had been able
to grasp even less than his Jewish brother could grasp of
the story of Jesus' life and death ; for there were racial
barriers standing between him and Jesus the Jew. And he
had other drawbacks. An exalted *Lord* was, for him, a
Figure even more vague and undefined than was the
Figure of the *Messiah* for the Jew. " It may be said with
certainty that at the time when Christianity originated,
Lord was a divine predicate intelligible to the whole
Eastern world." [1] Yes, and because so widely intelligible,
therefore undefined. For a *Lord* might be anything—
Adonis, Serapis, Mithras, or even the Roman Emperor
who was designated *Dominus et Deus*. And this lack of
definition in the Figure of the *Lord* invited accretions to it
from questionable sources. The Gentile convert had
round him, in his workaday life, comrades who still
worshipped one or other of these " Lords many," [2] and
welcomed the addition to their particular *Lord* of any
attractive feature, from whatever source ; indeed, there
was a kind of free-trade in divine attributes established
between the various Worships of the time. And so, since
the Gentile convert could transform his rather vague
conception of his Christian *Lord* into something vitally
and securely Christian, only by that same movement of

[1] Deissmann, *Light from the Ancient East*, p. 350.
[2] 1 Cor. viii. 5.

thought back to the Jesus of history of which we have
spoken, and since, further, that movement of thought
would be a more or less lengthy process, the question
arises, what was there to ensure that, meantime, he might
not be led away by the prevailing fashion of his time into
mythical and distorting speculations about his *Lord*?
Clearly, his Christian thought was in need of anchorage.
Where was that anchorage found?

It must be evident that the Lord's Supper, as celebrated
in Gentile churches where it was a memorial of the death
of Jesus, provided just such an anchorage. Let it be
remembered—and this is very important—that we are
dealing now with a time when, it is practically certain, no
written records of the life of Jesus were yet current in the
hands of believers, and when they had to depend upon
oral instruction for their knowledge of him. Also, it is
very unlikely that oral instruction could have been, at this
stage, and particularly in remoter places, so efficiently
organised and systematised as to be adequate, by itself,
for the control and safeguarding of the converts' processes
of thought. In such circumstances, the Lord's Supper
must have rendered invaluable service. For when the
believer sat at his Lord's table, his thoughts were constrained to move in the desired direction, back to Jesus.
Through moving symbolism, they were focused upon the
death on the cross and upon the person of him who had
endured that death. And not only so. That death was,
in itself, peculiarly challenging to the thought of a Gentile.
For although he was quite at home with the thought of a
dying god—could he not tell of several gods who had died?
Was not the grave of Zeus himself still to be seen in Crete?
—yet he was far from being at home with the thought of
this death. For this was no mythical death. It was the
real death of a real man. There had been a time when he
had laughed at the whole thing as sheer foolishness; [1]
and even now, it remained a paradox. And so, while the
Lord's Supper kept his thought directed upon the death,

[1] 1 Cor. i. 23.

the death itself kept insistently throwing it back upon the One who had endured it. Who was this man ? What manner of man could he have been that he was willing so to die ? And what manner of Being that his death should have borne such precious fruit ? Once a week at least, probably much oftener than that, Christian thought was constrained to take this direction. We must regard it as a fact of the most decisive importance that, through the Lord's Supper, the thought of the whole Gentile Church was kept steadily circling round the person of Jesus, and was continually being stimulated to a sense of wonder and to a zest for knowledge regarding him.

The Lord's Supper has been described as " the earliest *Gospel*." It was already *showing forth*,[1] or *proclaiming*, or *telling the story of* the death of the Lord Jesus, years before the first three Gospels were circulating in the hands of believers ; and it kept their faith and their thought in a close touch with his Person. Day after day, it opened a way for him into the inmost mind of the Church, with the result that he left his indelible stamp upon the plastic thought of that decisive and formative period. In no small measure it is because of this that to-day, after nearly two thousand years of the most varied experience, the Church's thought everywhere is still directing itself to the same Jesus, the Lord Jesus of history ; and an outstanding Christian thinker is able to say, in words that would find an echo from every Communion of Christendom :

" When we receive Holy Communion, we express our belief that the mysterious divine presence of which we are conscious in prayer is not only God, or the Spirit of God, but the Spirit of Jesus. . . . We are identifying the living well-spring of our faith, the source of our hope and our happiness, the guide and inspirer of our lives, with a historical character who lived nearly two thousand years ago." [2]

[1] 1 Cor. xi. 26.
[2] W. R. Inge, *Speculum Animæ*, p. 17.

APPENDIX A

WRITINGS OF THE SUB-APOSTOLIC AGE

A BRIEF account is here added of certain books referred to in this work. The more important of these were contemporaneous in their origin with later portions of the N.T. ; while some of them, like *1 Clement, Hermas, Barnabas*, and the *Didachê*, were candidates for inclusion in the N.T. Canon, and were for long read in churches alongside of the *Gospels* and the *Epistles of Paul*. Though they are important and valuable documents, we cannot but assent to the wisdom which guided the Church in the end to refuse them a permanent place in that high company.

THE " DIDACHÊ "

The *Didachê*, or " *Teaching* of the Apostles," as its fuller title runs, was discovered only in 1875, at Constantinople ; though its existence, and even some of its contents, had been known from references in the literature of the early centuries. Its discovery marked an epoch in the study of Primitive Christianity.

It contains sixteen short chapters, and may be described as a *Manual of Church Instruction*. There are two distinct parts in it: the first, chapters i.–vi., called the *Two Ways* (the Way of Life, and the Way of Death), is explicitly stated to be a manual of instruction for candidates for Baptism ; while the succeeding part contains instructions as to the conduct of Worship, Baptism, Fasting, the Eucharist, the position, or function, or proper treatment of Apostles, Prophets, Bishops, and Deacons ; and it closes with a chapter of warning and encouragement, based on the apocalyptic hope. The first part expounds the principles of Christian conduct, and is widely agreed to have been based on a manual originally used in the Jewish religion for the instruction of proselytes. The purpose of the whole work was evidently to provide guidance for churches which were in uncertainty owing to the lack of an established ministry ; and for this purpose the work set down what was regarded as the *Teaching* handed down from the Apostles.

Nothing is known as to the authorship of the *Didachê*. Most probably it originated in Syria, perhaps in Antioch itself. Attempts have been made to discredit its value as a witness for early practice, on the alleged ground that it can only have emanated from some remote, out-of-the-way locality, and should not therefore be taken as representative of any widespread condition of things. Scholarly opinion is growingly adverse to this view. Streeter, for instance, shows that " the influence of this little book on the later literature dealing with Church Order has been perhaps greater than that of any other work outside the New Testament." " It hovered on the verge of acceptance into the Canon until the fourth century." The book enjoyed " exceptional prestige," and must have been accepted, almost from the first, as " Apostolic in character, if not in actual authorship."

As to the date of its composition, external evidence is against a date much later than A.D. 100. Between 90 and 110 is the generally accepted date.

There is a very large literature on the *Didachê*. One of the most recent of the briefer studies of date and origin may be found in Streeter, *The Primitive Church*, pp. 279–287. A more extended, and easily accessible account is Vernon Bartlet's in Hastings' *Dictionary of the Bible*, the extra volume.

1 Clement

This is a long Letter, or Epistle, of sixty-five chapters, written by the Church at Rome to the Church at Corinth. In that old storm-centre, trouble and disunion had again broken out, resulting in the deposition of certain Presbyters ; and the Church at Rome writes, expostulating upon this uprising against constituted authority, and tendering counsel and guidance to the disrupted church.

Clement's name does not appear in the Epistle, which claims to be a message from the Roman church ; but tradition has consistently attributed the writing of it to Clement, and there is no good reason to question the tradition. The name of Clement appears in the episcopal lists as the third or fourth Bishop at Rome, towards the end of the first century. From

other sources we infer that he was a man of recognised emin-
ence.

The date of his writing lies within the limits A.D. 75 and 110.
There is wide agreement that the actual date was 96, the time
of Domitian's persecution. "The Epistle of Clement is usually,
and I believe correctly, dated A.D. 96 " (Streeter, *op. cit.* p.
189).

The Epistles of Ignatius

These also are highly important documents for our period.
Ignatius was the third Bishop at Antioch in Syria. A man
of strong personality and fervid zeal, he was condemned to be
sent to Rome, there to be killed by beasts in the Amphi-
theatre. On his journey to Rome as a prisoner, he passed
through the Christian regions in Asia Minor ; and while he
was halting at Smyrna, he wrote letters to the churches at
Ephesus, Magnesia, Tralles, and Rome. Then later, on
reaching Troas, he wrote to the Philadelphians, Smyrnæans,
and to Polycarp, the Bishop at Smyrna. He thanks each
church for the kindness they have shown him—the Church at
Rome, not yet reached, is begged to do nothing towards saving
his life and so denying him the crown of martyrdom ; and
counsels are given to the Asiatic churches, bidding them
strengthen their loyalty to their Bishop and Presbyters,
warning them against certain heresies, and bespeaking their
sympathy and help for his own orphaned church at Antioch.

The date of his martyrdom at Rome is given elsewhere as
A.D. 108. The exact date is doubtful ; but there is no ground
for rejecting the tradition that he was martyred at Rome
during the reign of Trajan (A.D. 98–117).

2 Clement

This is almost certainly of different authorship from
1 Clement. It is a Sermon, rather than an Epistle, inculcating
a pure life, a belief in the resurrection of the flesh, and an
exalted doctrine of Christ. The date is uncertain—somewhere
between A.D. 120 and 170. About 150 is often accepted as the
probable date. It may have emanated from Alexandria in
Egypt.

Epistle of Polycarp to the Philippians

Polycarp was Bishop at Smyrna, and became a martyr there,
probably in A.D. 155, at the age of eighty-six. He was, in his

person, the most important link of continuity between the Age of the great Apostles and the end of the second century. (Lightfoot, *Apostolic Fathers*, II. i. 458 f.)

His *Letter* to the Philippians is the only one of his letters that has been preserved to us. Its immediate purpose was to act as a covering letter for a collection of the *Letters of Ignatius* which Polycarp was sending to the Philippians soon after Ignatius' martyrdom, in response to their request that he should secure these for them. Polycarp takes the opportunity to counsel the Philippians against certain disorders in their church, and against the danger of apostasy.

The Epistle of Barnabas

This was reputed to be the work of Barnabas, the companion of Paul ; but little reliance can be placed in this tradition. The Epistle itself—more strictly it is a Homily—makes no claim to have been written by an Apostle ; and, if the writer's name was really *Barnabas*, he evidently thought himself well enough known to his probable readers to dispense with the need for further indicating his identity. There are reasons for believing that the place of origin was Alexandria, and there are none for connecting it with any other place. There is great uncertainty as to its date. The limits lie between the two great dates in the history of Jerusalem, A.D. 70 and 132. Lightfoot, Ramsay, and Bartlet accept a date soon after 70 ; others postpone it to the second century. The main purpose of the work is to give warnings against a Judaistic conception of the O.T. ; and it provides many examples of the more extreme application of allegory to the interpretation of the ancient Scriptures—a method of exegesis which was particularly favoured in Alexandria.

" The Shepherd " of Hermas

The *Shepherd* ranks with the *Apocalypse of John* as a survival of the prophetism of the N.T. Age ; though there is a wide difference between " the mediocrity of the timid little Greek and the fiery brilliance of the impassioned Jew." It was an exceedingly popular work during the early centuries, and was rejected from the Canon only at the last. Its popularity was due probably to its being a work which reflects the " simplicity and genuine piety of the rank and file of the average church members." It was written somewhere about the year

A.D. 100. There would never have been much doubt about this but for a reference to the work in a later fragmentary list of books of the Canon of the N.T., according to which it should be dated about the middle of the second century. It is highly probable that the list was in error, and that the correct date is approximately A.D. 100 (Streeter, *op. cit.* pp. 203–213).

Two other important witnesses, often referred to in this work, call for notice:

JUSTIN THE MARTYR

See Introduction. Justin wrote a second *Apology*, addressed to the Roman Senate; also a *Dialogue with Trypho the Jew*, which professes to be the record of an actual two days' disputation held at Ephesus.

PLINY'S LETTER TO TRAJAN (Ep. x. 97)

Pliny had been appointed the Roman Governor of the Province of Pontus and Bithynia by the Emperor Trajan, with whom he maintained an intimate official correspondence —fortunately preserved to us—during the fifteen months or so of his tenure of that high post. His famous letter to the Emperor about the Christians in his Province was called forth by the need for a clearer policy in dealing with this growing problem. In seeking Trajan's guidance, he explains what his method of procedure hitherto has been. When persons were accused of being Christians, he made inquiry whether they were so or not. If they confessed to being Christians, they were asked a second and third time, with a threat of punishment. If they remained obdurate in their confession, they were put to death. Those who denied that they were Christians he released, on their calling upon the gods of Rome and cursing Christ. He further reports of certain apostates from the faith whom he examined:

> " They asserted that this was the sum and substance of their fault or their error; namely, that they were in the habit of meeting before dawn on a stated day and singing alternately (*secum invicem*) a hymn to Christ as to a god, and that they bound themselves by an oath, not to the commission of any wicked deed, but that they would abstain from theft and robbery and adultery, that

they would not break their word, and that they would not withhold a deposit when reclaimed. This done, it was their practice, so they said, to separate, and then to meet together again for a meal, which however was of the ordinary kind and quite harmless. But even from this they had desisted after my edict, in which in pursuance of your commands I had forbidden the existence of clubs (hetærias)."—See Lightfoot, *Apostolic Fathers*, II. i. 13–21.

APPENDIX B

A LIST OF BOOKS CONSULTED AND FOUND USEFUL IN THE PREPARATION OF THIS WORK

GENERAL

Weiss, J. . . . *Das Urchristentum.* 1917.

Harnack, A. . . *Die Mission und Ausbreitung des Christentums.* 1902. Eng. Trans., 1904.

Bousset, W. . . *Die Religion des Judentums.* 1926.
Kyrios Christos. 1913. 2nd ed., 1921.

Streeter, B. H. . . *The Primitive Church.* 1929.

Deissmann, A. . . *St. Paul.* 1926.
Light from the Ancient East. 1922.

Dobschuetz, E. von *Christian Life in the Primitive Church.* 1904.

Scott, E. F. . . *The Beginnings of the Church.* 1914.
The Gospel and its Tributaries. 1928.
The New Testament To-day. 1921.
The Epistle to the Hebrews. 1922.

Dill, S. . . . . *Roman Society from Nero to Marcus Aurelius.* 1904.

Foakes-Jackson . *The Rise of Gentile Christianity.* 1927.

Hoskyns and Davey *The Riddle of the New Testament.* 1931.

Holl, K. . . . . *Gesammelte Aufsaetze zur Kirchengesch.,* II. Der Osten. 1927.

Norden, E. . . . *Agnostos Theos.* 1913.

Welch, A. C. . . *Visions of the End.* 1922.

Angus, S. . . . *The Mystery Religions of Christianity.* 1925.
Religious Quests of the Græco-Roman World. 1929.

Scott, C. A. A. . . *Christianity according to St. Paul.* 1927.
The Fellowship of the Spirit. 1921.

Lake, K. . . . *Earlier Epistles of St. Paul.* 1911.

Montefiore, C. G. . *Judaism and St. Paul.* 1914.

Gardner, P. . . . *The Religious Experience of St. Paul.* 1911.

Pratt, J. B. . . . *The Religious Consciousness.* 1920.

Moffatt, J. . . . *Love in the New Testament.* 1929.

Rawlinson, A. E. J. *The New Testament Doctrine of the Christ.* 1926.

Mackintosh, H. R. . *The Person of Jesus Christ.* 1913.

Lohmeyer, E. . . *Kyrios Jesus.* 1928.

Morgan, W. . . *The Religion and Theology of Paul.* 1917.
The Nature and Right of Religion. 1926.

Williams, Lukyn . *The Hebrew-Christian Messiah.* 1916.

Andrews, H. T. . *The Christ of Apostolic Faith.* 1929.

Bacon, B. W. . . *Jesus and Paul.* 1921.
The Story of Jesus. 1927.

Bindley, T. H. . . *Religious Thought in Palestine in the Time of Christ.* 1931.

Bartlet, J. V. . . *The Apostolic Age, its Life, Doctrine, Worship, and Polity.* 1900.

BOOKS BEARING MORE SPECIFICALLY ON WORSHIP

Gunkel, H. . . . *Die Wirkungen des Heiligen Geistes.* 1909.

Scott, E. F. . . *The Spirit in the New Testament.* 1923.

Oesterley, W. O. E. *The Jewish Background of the Christian Liturgy.* 1925.

Oesterley and Box . *Religion and Worship of the Jewish Synagogue.* 1907.

Lietzmann, H. . . *Messe und Herrenmahl.* 1926.
Geschichte der Alten Kirche, i. 1932.

Brilioth, Y. . . *Eucharistic Faith and Practice.* 1930.

Hunkin, J. W. . . *Chap. I. of The Evangelical Doctrine of Holy Communion.* 1930.

Macgregor, G. H. C. *Eucharistic Origins.* 1928.

Warren, F. E. . . *The Liturgy and Ritual of the Ante-Nicene Church.* 1912.

Heitmueller, W. . *Taufe und Abendmahl bei Paulus.* 1903.
Im Namen Jesu. 1903.

Duchesne, L. . . *Christian Worship, Its Origins and Evolution.* 1923.

Brightman, F. E. . *Liturgies, Eastern and Western.* 1896.

Wetter, G. P. . . *Altchristliche Liturgien — Das Christl. Mysterium.* 1921.

Guardini, R. . . *Vom Geist der Liturgie.* 1922.

Baumstark, A. . . . *Vom Geschichtlichen Werden der Liturgie.*
1923.

Drews, P. . . . *Studien zur Gesch. des Gottesdienstes,*
ii. and iii. 1906.

Duhm, A. . . . *Gottesdienst im aeltesten Christentum.*
1928.

Bouquet, A. C. . . *The Real Presence.* 1928.

Sperry, W. L. . . *Reality in Worship.* 1927.

Chase, F. H. . . *The Lord's Prayer in the Early Church.*
1923.

Kroll, J.. . . . *Die Christl. Hymnodik bis zu Klemens von
Alexandreia.* 1921.

Stephen, Caroline . *Quaker Strongholds.* 1911.

Linton, A. . . . *Twenty-five Consecration Prayers.* 1921.

Simpson, R. S. . . *Ideas in Corporate Worship.* 1927.

Harnack, A. . . *Bible Reading in the Early Church.* 1912.

Heiler, F. . . . *Das Gebet.* 1922.
The Spirit of Worship. 1926.

Von der Goltz, E. F. *Das Gebet in der aeltesten Christenheit.*
1901.

TRANSLATIONS

The Apostolic Fathers. By K. Lake (Loeb Classical Library).
The Apocryphal New Testament. By M. R. James.

COMMENTARIES, ETC., SPECIALLY USEFUL

I Corinthians. By J. Weiss, in Meyer's *Commentary.*
Revelation. By E. Lohmeyer, in *Handbuch zum N.T.*
Apostolic Fathers. By J. B. Lightfoot.
Didaché, in Hastings' *Dictionary of the Bible.* By J. Vernon
Bartlet.

INDEX OF SUBJECTS

15

INDEX OF NEW TESTAMENT REFERENCES

PRINTED BY MORRISON AND GIBB LTD., EDINBURGH AND LONDON

264
m13

LINCOLN CHRISTIAN UNIVERSITY

14263

3 4711 00224 5050